NO ENTRY

Examining The
Powers That
Undermine Our
Full Potential

COLBER PROSPER, M.S.

NO ENTRY

ISBN- 978-0-692-86362-6

Copyright © 2017
Colber Prosper

Printed by CreateSpace, an Amazon.com Company @ www.createspace.com

Book cover: www.pearlio.com

Edited by: "My Team"

Graphic Image: https://images.google.com

Printed in the United States of America

Believing in the impossible isn't just a past time but essential for survival. We have to become our own superheroes saving ourselves, our future selves, our communities and dreams. The band The Script has a great song titled Superheroes. The lyrics to their chorus is,

> *When you've been fighting for it all your life You've been struggling to make things right That's how a superhero learns to fly Every day, every hour Turn the pain into power*

Like in this song we must turn our pains and struggles into power. However, we can't do it alone. We must help each other. If we work together and believe in something greater, we can begin tapping into our greater selves.

These are my love notes to the oppressed.

Table of Content

Forward

Power, like the free market, is the invisible hand that moves all of us. It weighs on our mind as we try to figure out how to get more of it, consciously and unconsciously. This book will provide an overview of how power structures are organized, and how they exert their force on people and communities, in particular, those that are most vulnerable.

As you read this analysis, consider the losses that we incur by allowing those with power to use it inappropriately. Consider that those losses are socialized to all of us if we don't all start to recognize how the power structures impact us and our future. Let's reflect and change course as Prosper suggests.

-Carlos Gutierrez, MBA
Entrepreneur, Catalyst, Chief TroubleMaker

Chapter One

Introduction

I was on a school break and decided to go to South Florida to see my family. During this time at home my father and I watched a movie. In the movie one of the characters was a poor black teenage male who was struggling in life, but showed promising talents and skills. He had potential! The hero in the movie was a middle class, middle age, white male, who, while working to solve a case of related murders throughout the city, found himself in the library looking at historical documents as part of his investigation. Although he began with a computer search, you could tell he lacked computer skills. The black teenager went over and helped the hero find the newspaper articles that reported similar murders, years past. At that moment, my father in the most encouraging voice said to the TV screen, "Go young man!" And people wonder why I speak out in movies and at the television, lol. I told my dad, "It's not that easy." Reflecting on my college courses and the books and articles I had read, I thought about the papers I wrote on discrimination and components of institutional racism. I continued, "There are societal forces that will hold him back." And, I will never forget my dad's response. He simply said, "Should I tell him to give up?" I had no answer. We finished the movie but my dad's words have never left me.

My father's response reminds me of a quote by Mary Oliver, an award winning American poet. In her poem, *Evidence*, Oliver writes, "Keep some room in your heart for the unimaginable."[1] My father's response embodied this quote. To think the black young man from the movie could become successful and actually reach his full potential was hoping and wishing for the unimaginable. And even though it was a movie, the young male's fate was synonymous with the lives of a significant percentage of young men of color in our reality. The barriers and institutions he must have faced to succeed were practically impossible. But my father was hoping this fictional character would succeed. Moreover, knowing my father, he took it a step further. He left room in his own heart to believe the unimaginable. I know this to be true because my father and mother raised my brothers, sisters and myself with this in their hearts.

"Keep some room in your heart for the unimaginable" is the last line of Mary Oliver's poem.[2] And when I read the poem in its entirety I find she writes about what beauty is and where beauty lies. The flowers and waters are beautiful but also different. A flower and a body of water have their own purposes but the central purpose of beauty is to excite its spectators. The poem moved from the beauty of the physical world to the beauty of people. The beauty of people can be recognized not only by their physical details but also by their characteristics like

---

[1] Mary Oliver, *Evidence* (Boston: Beacon Press, 2009), 43.
[2] Ibid., 43

strength and curiosity. This capacity within people is beautiful itself. She writes that the body, "is the only vessel in the world that can hold, in a mix of power and sweetness: words, song, gesture, passion, ideas, ingenuity, devotion, merriment, vanity and virtue."[3] Consistent with Poet Oliver's artistic expression, I can feel very bleak about the current situation of those in our society we have discarded, marginalized and kept in a system of oppression. Nevertheless, within my own body, I too, believe in the unimaginable and such a thing is beautiful and worth fighting for.

And, in my own life I have always fought for the unimaginable. I have fought for success and for reaching my full potential. There weren't many things that came easy for me or for many people I know. Along with the people in my village we have fought for everything that we have accomplished. Oh, to be clear, when I use the term village I am talking about my family, extended family, close friends, church families and anyone with whom I have spent significant time. In my life, I have had to constantly persevere or in Haitian Creole, "I had to have a la fin." A la fin in Haitian creole means perseverance, but I think it also means having faith in knowing you will be successful in the end. This is what my family and my home churches taught me. In my journey towards upward mobility, I experienced forces designed to slow me down and at times ones that almost derailed me. I've witnessed

---

[3] Ibid.

4

these same forces derail so many of my friends and students I worked with. And, I have seen so much promise and potential in so many individuals and then witnessed that promise and potential extinguished or relinquished because of oppressive forces.

Society leads you to believe that it's up to the individual to reach his/her/zirs promise and potential, and that it is the individual's responsibility to recognize their potential and to cultivate it. If a person doesn't reach their potential, then it's that individual's fault. This person didn't work hard enough, didn't make the right decisions or even sabotaged their own success. Our fundamental belief in a capitalist society is meritocracy. People have the things they have in life solely based on hard work and their good intentions. People make money based on their talents, skills, knowledge and experience. If you don't make a lot money or have a fancy title then you don't have much skill, talent and etc. You are not worth much and that is your fault. But what if I told you that wasn't the whole truth? What if I told you that the larger society plays a role in your potential and you achieving it? Would you believe me?

Purpose aka the Point

My purpose in writing this book is to show how these societal "forces" which can be identified as power can affect people's everyday lives and overall life trajectory. My perspective is informed by multiple disciplines. I hold a Bachelor's in History with a minor in Political Science and a Master's in College Student Personnel. Therefore, I will use history, political science, higher education and research from various fields to support my claims. I will also share my own experience, which not only inform this work but also influence the way I present it.

I come from several subcultures. And, I come from the depths of oppression. I choose to write in a way to show and represent the many facets of my identity. I am formally educated having attended reputable higher educational institutions. Therefore, my arguments will be based on research and history. I identify as Haitian African American and will use Haitian Creole, Standard English and African American English or vernacular in this book. I'll be explaining terminology, theories and certain ideas in the standard or also known as the queen/king English form. Moreover, I will switch to a more conversational tone using African American English throughout the book. Please do not mistake the switching of vernaculars and language as grammatical errors but as an intentional representation of the cultures I identify with. This is critical because language constructs thought and outlook on life.[4] So, I can't fully explain me and fully accept myself if I can't write in the languages and dialects I use throughout my own life. This is how I interact with the world.

---

[4] Geneva Gay, *Culturally Responsive Teaching Theory, Research, and Practice* (New York: Teachers College Press, 2000), 80.

I am also a millennial who loves music and will use songs to make a point and/or to depict an idea. I come from a working/middle class family and will show how classism affected our daily lives. I am a person with learning disabilities and because of this I have kept this book short and to the point, reasoning that those like me won't be discouraged by the number of pages. I am an entrepreneur and business person and will share those experiences. I am a spiritual being who believes in a higher power, and I will share how this gave and gives me hope and so much more. I also care about our environment and how we use natural resources. I am these and so much more. I am sick of being labeled, told who and what I am and placed in the box. I define me! I will tell you and the world who I am. And these are my experiences.

But, I'll tell you right now that this book ain't for everybody and that's fine. The hip-hop artist Big Krit said this in his song *Mt. Olympus*, what I'm cooking ain't meant for your kind.[5] No hard feelings if this book doesn't vibe with you. I still love ya. Nevertheless, this book is for people like me and/or who feel me. This is for people who are wanting more, more in the sense of finding and/or exploring themselves. These people want, have imagined, or have seen a glimpse, a shadow of their better selves. They are open to different thoughts and ideas. They are

---

[5] Big KRIT, "Mt. Olympus," *Genius,* https://genius.com/Big-krit-mt-olympus-lyrics.

looking for answers. They are looking for guidance. They are looking for themselves.

Above all else this book is a discussion between me and you. The written style of this book is inspired by my cultures and their emphasis placed on speaking, word play, creativity and being a charismatic orator. The art of bringing the speaking voice to literature is done so well by the famous Ghanaian writer Ama Ata Aidoo and I follow her footsteps. I will be presenting to you my ideas and asking you questions as if we are talking to each other. I'm gonna be open and honest and I hope you can do the same for me but most importantly for yourself. Our discussion will continue via social media. Within the private places of our minds to the open spaces of social media we will explore who we are, where we come from and where we wanna go.

Finally, I wrote this book because I believe in the unimaginable. I believe all people, if given the right support, can reach their full potential. What motivated me to write this book is that I have witnessed the constant death of human potential. It's the dying on the inside I can no longer bear to see and do nothing about. Once a person has given up on zir dreams, and cease trying to obtain zir potential, what more does that person have to live for? Is that person even alive? As part of the human race what is my responsibility in the widespread global deaths of human potential? I believe we all are connected and it's my responsibility to figure out why such atrocities continue to exist. In the next following pages, I will explain how power contributes to the death of so much human potential. And, I will show how power plays a significant role in our lives, our choices, the environment and our potential. My purpose is to bring about awareness and change.

Chapter Two

Power

"Now how can one man have all that power"[6] -Young Jeezy

Power and Players

The quote above is by the hip-hop artist Young Jeezy. In this explicit song Jeezy talks about all his benefits, rewards, access and about a person who saw him having so much power. Jeezy's power leads the person to ask the question – "How can one man have all that power?" Jeezy makes a great point because we all should be asking ourselves, "How does an individual, group, organization and society acquire their power?" In this chapter, we will explore this idea.

Kanye West, another hip-hop artist, writes in his song *Power*, "No one man should have all that power."[7] This is one of my favorite songs by Kanye because he talks about the system and how social structures are being directed. He talks about schools being closed across the country and about prisons being opened, while shedding light on private prisons and the prison industrial complex. Those in power have the power to open and close social

---

[6] Young Jeezy, "Hell You Talkin Bout," *AZ Lyrics*,
http://www.azlyrics.com/lyrics/youngjeezy/hellyoutalkinbout.html.
[7] Kanye West, "Power," *Genius,* https://genius.com/Kanye-west-power-lyrics.

institutions like schools and prisons at will. I do believe Kanye is right, "No one man should have all that power."[8]

When I was in graduate school expressing my concerns to one of my mentors Dr. Fritz Polite, I was telling him my feelings of the racist acts that took place on campus and how the institution wasn't doing all that it could to support minority students. Dr. Polite then tells me, "You all (students) must understand power and how power works." I thought to myself, Doc I'm talking about racism and you're talking about power. And "omg" here comes one of his stories lol. I didn't get what we were saying at the time but I was wise enough to take his advice. In the coming years after that conversation I spent my free time reading about power and how power works. I see now what Dr. Polite was talking about. So, what is power? To put it simply, power is the capacity to get your desired outcome. Your ability to get what you want.

There are many definitions of power from a plethora of fields like political science, philosophy, and economics. Thinking about power from multiple disciplines intrigues me so much that I take this same approach with my work. In the college courses I teach, I take a multiple disciplinary approach to give my students a more holistic perspective of the course content. This enhances critical thinking and problem solving. In my consulting firm, Prosper & Partners, LLC, which develops innovative solutions for professionals and organizations, we also use a multiple

---

[8] Ibid.

disciplinary approach. Our network of 20+ consultants who work in different fields and sectors enable us to be in the nexus of social innovation. Subsequently, we have assisted our clients and partners to create more comprehensive solutions for their complex problems. We have worked with government agencies like the Federal Department of Education and the Environmental Protection Agency. We have assisted countless organizations and communities across the United States and in other countries in community building. This involves bringing individuals, groups and agencies together to work more effectively with one another to address the major issues that affect them. And in all of my work here in the United States and abroad I have dealt with power being used for or against our clients and partners.

The definition of power that suits our purpose comes from the field of political science. Political science professor Dr. Thomas Magstadt writes power is, "the capacity to influence or control the behavior of persons and institutions, whether by persuasion or coercion."[9] Magstadt, writing about individual and institutional behavior, discusses personal behavior because people's behaviors can be measured, controlled, and analyzed. This is a major point I will focus on in the next chapter. Finally, Dr. Magstadt shares that power is achieved by the means of persuasion and coercion, which helps us identify when

---

[9] Thomas Magstadt: *Understanding Politics Ideas, Institutions, and Issues* (Belmont: Wadsworth Cengage Learning, 2009), 696.

and why power is used. We will find, by the end of this text, that there are several means in which power is channeled.

Again, power is the capacity to get your desired outcome. Therefore, everybody has it. Think when a parent asks their child to do something and the child does it, that parent is using their power. This is what we call individual power. When a group of friends convinces a friend to do something that's group power. When an organization or governing body tells people to do something and the people comply, this is institutional power. Now that we understand power we need to know its capacities in terms of its range and depths.

Dr. Steven Lukes, a political and social theorist does a great job explaining what power is and its different levels. He calls these levels "dimensions."[10] In his book, *Power*, he explains how power is used and to what degree.

One such question is: 'Who can adversely affect the interest of whom? This question, focusing on effects upon interests, can be interpreted in various ways, and indeed contending inter-pretations of it have generated one of the more lively debates about power in recent years, centering mainly around the literature of community power studies, beginning with Floyd Hunter's Community Power Structure and Dahl's study of New Haven, Who Governs? On what I have called the one-dimensional view of power,

---

[10] Steven Lukes, introduction to *Power*, ed. Steven Lukes (New York: New York University Press, 1986), 9.

interests are seen as equivalent to revealed preferences –
revealed, that is, by political behavior in decision-making;
to exercise power is to prevail over the contrary
preferences of others, with respect to 'key issues'. (This is
the view that Dahl puts to work in Who Governs?, though
it is only distantly related to his definition of power cited
above.) On the two-dimensional view of power advanced
by Peter Bachrach and Morton Baratz, one exercises
power in the manner the one dimensionalist favours, but
also by controlling the agenda, mobilizing the bias of the
system, determining which issues are 'key' issues, indeed
which issues come up for decision, and excluding those
which threaten the interests of the powerful. Here interests
adversely affected are shown by politically expressed
preferences and extra-political or covertly expressed
grievances and demands that are, in various ways, denied
entry into decision-making process. The three-
dimensional view incorporates power of the first and two
kinds, but also allows that power may operate to shape and
modify desires and beliefs in a manner contrary to
people's interests. In consequence, neither revealed
preferences nor grievances and inchoate demands will
always express them. Our earlier discussion of interests
helps clarify this possibility. Power, on this view, may
encourage and sustain attitudes and expectations that work
against people's 'welfare interests' or subvert and thwart
their pursuit of their ulterior, focal aim, or both.[11]

---

[11] Ibid., 9.

Lukes sees power operating in three different ways or dimensions: 1) Issue 2) Agenda 3) Manipulation.[12] Issue, the first dimension, is pushing your interest on key issues over others. Agenda, the second dimension, is creating a context and agenda to get what you want, rather than others getting what they need or want. Manipulation, the third dimension, is manipulating people to do what you want even it if hurts them. Remember the acronym "I AM" for Issue, Agenda and Manipulation. Each dimension has multiple components. Therefore, they're not simplistic but have their own operating structure and system. People can pull different components from one or more dimension of power to achieve what they want. This all begins with the interests; the things people and institutions want. He echoed my sentiments above that power in its simplest form is pushing for one's interests but he clearly makes the point that power is pushing his/her/zirs own interest over others.

To further summarize and explain Lukes' writing I will use a personal example. When I was younger my siblings and I would fight over the TV. This is because we would break them or open them to see what's inside. So, to punish us my parents only allowed us to watch one TV in the house. Having one TV as the eldest in the house I used my age and my physical stature over my siblings to watch the programs I wanted. I used my individual power. The TV became a key issue and I told my siblings what I

---

[12] Changing Minds, "The Three Face of Power," *Changing Minds,* http://www.changingminds.org/explanations/power/three_faces.htm.

wanted and I placed my interests over theirs. This is Lukes' first dimension.

The second dimension of power is agenda. Remember the second dimension also includes the first dimension. The additional components found in this dimension are controlling what interests get to be talked about, deciding on the issues that are "really important," mobilizing a "system" that upholds certain interests and making sure that system excludes anything that could disrupt the interest of those in power.[13] Back to my example I would tell my siblings how certain television programs like football were important. I told them it was crucial for us to watch it instead of their favorite cartoon programs because football was real and I wanted to play organized football in the future. I would discuss TV rights when our parents weren't home so I could remain in control. I would then tell my siblings not to say anything to our parents because they didn't need to know and they were too busy. I tried to exclude anything that would jeopardize my control of the TV. I'm trying to tell you the TV situation was real lol.

Lukes' final dimension, manipulation not only has material ramifications but also psychological. He wrote that the third dimension incorporates the first two and has components that take power even further. The best way to explain this dimension is its results. The results of this dimension of power change people's beliefs and desires

---

[13] Lukes, *Power*, 9.

so much so that their interests become the same as those in power even if those interests are actually bad for the people. In this dimension the more powerful can influence the thoughts of the less powerful. Telling my sister watching football was good for her was me trying to change her thoughts and desires. She did play flag football in high school but her real interests were writing, cosmetology and business. However, this is where my example stops short while this dimension continues. Dr. Lukes shares that in this dimension power may encourage and maintain the expectations that people not in positions of power are to work against their own "welfare interest."[14] Welfare interests can mean many things but at its basic level it can be your own interest in having good health. In this dimension those with less power will uphold the interest of those with more power, even if it's detrimental to their health. It's like me telling you, you shouldn't eat because I need to eat or you shouldn't try to better yourself because you should actually work on helping me better myself. Yea, it's real and this is happening every day.

Pause: How has power played out in your life?

Dominant Identities and Power

The way power is played out in the United States and in other countries is that those with the most power make and change the rules. These people are called the dominant

---

[14] Ibid., 6.

group. If you don't belong to the dominant group, you are categorized as a subordinate. "Dominant groups, by definition, set the parameters within which the subordinates operate. The dominant group holds the power and authority in society relative to the subordinates and determines how that power and authority may be acceptably used."[15] Now this isn't just the powerful versus the non-powerful, which depicts a binary, the idea that things in society have to be one thing or the other: e.g. black or white. Rather, it's a continuum where you have black on one side and white on the other and a ton of different shades of grays in the middle. This is because we all have some type of power and belong to different dominant and subordinate groups. Dr. Beverly Tatum, former President of Spelman College, writes

> People are commonly defined as other on the basis of race or ethnicity, gender, religion, sexual orientation, socioeconomic status, age, and physical or mental ability. Each of these categories has a form of oppression associated with it: racism, sexism, religious, oppression/ant-Semitism, heterosexism, classism, ageism, and ableism, respectively. In each case, there is a group considered dominant (systematically advantage by the society because of group membership) and a group considered subordinate or targeted

---

[15] Beverly Daniel Tatum: *"Why Are All the Black Kids Sitting Together in the Cafeteria?"* (New York: Basic Book, 2003), 23.

(systematically disadvantaged). When we think about our multiple identities, most of us will find that we are both dominant and targeted at the same time. But it is the targeted identities that hold our attention and the dominant identities that often go unexamined.[16]

Dr. Tatum clearly explains the different categories in society. Power has always been around in our society but the way that power is used has changed throughout history. Each category indicates a different way in which power is used and manipulated. And depending on who you are and what you identify with determines the type and of advantages you will get from society. Such advantages a person receives for just being a part of dominant groups are called privilege. I'll use myself as an example. I am a young heterosexual Haitian African American male who has learning disabilities, is Christian and from a working to middle class family. My dominant identity in the United States and certain places in the world is that I am a Christian. And, in the United States and the world my dominant groups are also male, able bodied, American, heterosexual and middle class. I don't think about these identities much because our institutions are structured to uphold, support and advance them. This is power. As a male I am socialized and rewarded for being a leader in the business sphere. However, a woman is less likely to be seen as leader and is expected to be a nurturer

---

[16] Tatum, *"Why Are All the Black Kids Sitting Together in the Cafeteria?,"* 22.

above all else.[17] Her leadership will be more in question and her qualifications will be tested more.

My subordinate identities in the United States and the world are that I am Haitian, young, black, have learning disabilities including dyslexia. My economic background can vary depending where I am in the world. I think about these identities often and some I think about every day. I have experienced and witnessed racial, ethnic, age and learning ability discrimination. Historically, blacks have been oppressed in the United States and other parts of the world. People have disregarded my Haitian culture and placed their own culture over mine. Because of my age people question my credibility and the credibility of my business, even though we have worked in seven different countries. I have been made fun of and ostracized for not learning somethings as quickly as my peers, although my difficulty learning new material was directly connected to my learning disabilities over, which I had no control. Those in power or the dominant groups control the rules, labels and systems that affect my subordinate identities. They dictate the landscape of society and how I should be perceived, treated and/or handled. They make sure that I do not inhibit them from reaching their goals and interests and that I actually help them achieve their goals even when they are a detriment to my own well-being.

Pause: What are your identities?

---

[17] Sheryl Sandbreg, *Lean in Women, Work, and The Will To Lead* (New York: Alfred A. Knopf, 2013), 43.

Power Working in Real Life

Now let's make this real and show the bigger picture. In this section I will give examples of how those with more power have used it to silence and/or oppress others. I'm going to begin with an early, personal issue and gradually move to a national, critical level.

When I started football camp, my freshmen year in college, our coaching staff was mostly white men. They upheld white middle class values and from my perspective only appreciated how the game looked and was played in decades' past. During camp the coaches told the incoming class that they wanted all players to look the same on the field. Anything like specialty socks, visors, "wearing excessive" wrist or armbands and taping of cleats were prohibited. This was quite a disappointment to me and some of my new friends on the team. This rule was not up for discussion and there was no compromise. We felt that this was a total disregard to our self-expression and the way we envisioned ourselves on the field. We were unable to tell our coaches that we took pride in the way we looked on the field and the places we came from valued the extra attention and details we placed into our uniforms. They didn't consider the football cultures we came from. I came from South Florida where the University of Miami (UM), the Hurricanes redefined football. The UM football team changed the way the game was played while looking stylish on the field. That's how I pictured myself looking and playing on the field. I complained about this rule to some of my teammates who were mostly white and not from Florida, and they made me feel bad for it. Most of them agreed with the coaching staff that it wasn't something we should discuss. My teammates and coaches didn't take the time to really understand where I was coming from. I didn't feel heard or understood. However, my experience was not unique. Researcher Mickey Melendez found that black male athletes at PWIs (Predominantly White Institutions) can experience mental health issues like paranoia and feelings of isolation because of double standards and misunderstandings.[18] Finally, I felt bad for even talking about the issue. I'm not saying that adding a little extra to your uniform was a black thing. There were white players that were upset about the rule too. What I am saying is that our mostly white coaching staff wanted to uphold their middle-class expectations of what football players should look like over their players' perspectives.

To analyze this in the first dimension of power, our coaches told us what their interests were and they put their interests over ours. Then they controlled the agenda about which topics we talked about. This is the expression of the second dimension. The topic was not up for discussion and it was over when they said it was over. Finally, the third dimension including the first two was the changing

[18] Mickey C. Melendez, "Black Football Players on a Predominantly White College Campus: Psychosocial and Emotional Realities of Black College Athlete Experience," Journal of Black Psychology 34, no. 4 (2008): 11, http://www.journals.sagepub.com/doi/pdf/10.1177/0095798408319874 (accessed July 30, 2016).

of desires. In the end, I felt bad for even talking about something I valued and condemned myself for being upset in the first place.

Organizational level

I received my Masters in College Student Personnel from one of the top programs in the nation. It is a higher educational administration degree that studies colleges, universities and students and I have worked at several institutions since obtaining my degree. Moreover, my company consults and conduct trainings and workshops in the field. While I was in grad school my professor, mentor and leading scholar, Dr. Terrell Strayhorn said colleges and universities are microcosms of our society. The higher educational institutions that I attended were HWIs (Historically White Institutions). These colleges and universities were created for and admit mostly educated white people. Therefore, the interests of white people were pushed, supported and satisfied while my interest or the interests of those who looked like me took a back seat.

To take it to the institutional level, I'll talk about my undergraduate institution as a whole. When I was a student there it was ranked in the top ten liberal arts private schools in the south. The number of enrolled students was little over a thousand. Whites students were the vast majority and the black students totaled about one hundred, give or take a few. The retention of black students was at a much lower rate than white students. Not only were Black students were more likely to leave the institution than white students, they also left with significant debt and few credits. The school wanted to better the retention of black students but didn't know how. During this time, several racial bias incidents took place on campus. It was so bad that the local media got involved. My friends and I wanted change. We wanted to make the campus more inclusive with more support for minority students to succeed. So, with the help of some faculty members and staff we did our research. We found that black students are most likely to be successful when interacting with faculty members that looked like them and shared similar cultural backgrounds.[19] This was good for white students as well because racial diversity increases their complex thinking.[20] They can also have a better understanding of cultural and racial differences which enhances their ability to interact with people different from themselves. We told the administration we wanted more faculty of color. The unforeseen backlash commenced after we started to mobilize on campus. I was the president of BSA (Black Student Association) and we were heavily criticized for wanting minority faculty. We were labeled as trouble makers and people said we did not appreciate the

---

[19] Douglas A. Guiffrida, "Othermothering as a Framework for Understanding African American Students' Definitions of Student-Centered Faculty," The Journal of Higher Education 76, no. 6 (2005): 718, doi https://doi.org/10.1353/jhe.2005.0041.
[20] Anthony Lising, Mitchell J. Chang, Kenji Hakuta, David A. Kenny, Shana Levin and Jeffrey F. Milem, "Effects of Racial Diversity on Complex Thinking in College Students," Sage Journals Psychological Science 15, no. 8 (2004): 509, doi https://doi.org/10.1111/j.0956-7976.2004.00710.x.

current campus community. We were treated even more differently and felt more like outcasts.

It was clear to my peers and me that the imagination of the campus community was limited. They could not fathom black and brown faculty walking around and teaching students. It was so foreign to them! Their interest was to continue the status quo. People asked us, "Why do you need black professors when we have such great professors already?" Yea, we had great professors, but I didn't always enjoy being put on the spot by my white professors when we talked about black people and I was expected to represent all the black people in the world. I wanted to rest assured that when my white peers made a racist comment that the professor would take care of it and not leave it to me as the only black student in class to address. That wasn't my job. Plus, I wanted to learn more about minorities and their contributions to the world in all of my subjects. I was tired of hearing about the same old white guys like Aristotle, Plato, John Locke, Immanuel Kant, etc.

I hope now you can start to see the three dimensions of power, issue, agenda and manipulation. The interest of the institution in keeping things the same was given a higher priority than our academic success. This is the first dimension. The second is that they made us feel like outcasts because we were disrupting their system. Finally, we were told that wanting such is thing is an insult to the current faculty and we should be ashamed of ourselves. I did feel bad because I had meaningful relationships with some of my white professors. I really questioned myself. But we stayed on course with the help and guidance of some faculty and staff. The response of our administration was that they didn't have the funds to carry out such diversity initiatives. However, the funds were then donated. By my senior year, we finally hired an African American female professor. But by then I had already lost most of my friends who were a part of the fight. They had left and didn't get to see the victory. Since 2008, my graduation year, that same professor has gained full tenured. This means she has all the rights and privileges of a professor at the institution. But, eight years later, she's still the only full time faculty member of color at the college. Nevertheless, the campus has changed over the years because of her and the other staff of color including their white allies. Overall, diversity and inclusion is a major issue for a lot of PWIs across the country. As student populations get more and more diverse, PWIs have to be more inclusive in their practices and the way they educate. If not, many will have to close their doors.

National Level aka Institutional Racism

In this section I will discuss #BlackLivesMatter, the international civil rights group and movement. I will focus on their work across in the United States. Because power dynamics are a lot more complicated on such a scale, I will begin by briefly reviewing American history, specifically concerning the construction of race. And, I will share the foundations of #BlackLivesMatter and law enforcement. I will then show how elites and law enforcement created and maintained a system that was designed to control black and brown people. Side note: the reference to black and brown people mean black people of African descent and Latino/as. Finally, I will use Lukes' theory to break down these systems of power.

#BlackLivesmatter is fighting the construction of race and the groups that have historically used racism to maintain their power. What I learned in school was that the pilgrims founded the new world and they wanted freedom from the tyranny of the British crown and freedom to practice their religions. What I didn't learn in grade school but I learned in college was that the major reason the first settlers left England for the new world was to make money. Christopher Columbus reported that these so called new lands had rich soil, resources and minerals like silver and gold. However, in 1607 the first British settlers to North America had a hard time growing anything on the lands and wouldn't have survived without the help of Native Americans.[21] It got so bad that our nation's first settlers had issues of cannibalism.[22] Yea, they don't teach us this in school. As time passed they were able to grow tobacco to sell to their British counterparts.

---

[21] Ronald Takaki, *A Different Mirror A History of Multicultural America* (New York: Little, Brown and Company, 1993), 34.
[22] Ibid.

This sparked a wave of immigration from England to North America. The English came to North America to own land and to farm for profit. To do this land owners needed help. So, they started to "recruit" others. Companies imported servants by kidnapping other whites like the Irish to bring to the new world. Once they made it to the new colonies they were placed into servitude. Colonists also tried to place Native Americans in servitude but that wasn't very successful because the Native Americans knew the lands and could flee to a nearby tribe. Elite land owners also imported Africans to serve as indentured servants. Around this time American slavery wasn't officially created. Elites would place whites and Africans in indentured servitude. This meant that they would work for very low wages or no wages for certain number of years and then be set free. During this time the white and black servants spent a lot of time with each other because of their work. These communities were not only bonded by work but with the bearing of children and the planning and implementation of rebellions.

The Bacon Rebellion led by Nathaniel Bacon, a white Virginia council member first started as a militia to fight Native Americans.[23] He then turned against the elites after the Governor of Virginia charged him with treason because he organized a militia of lower class whites. Blacks joined Bacon's army after he was classified as a rebel and they marched to Jamestown, VA and burned it

---

[23] Ibid., 63.

down in 1676.[24] Nevertheless, after this revolt, the elite devised a plan.

> Four years after Bacon's Rebellion, the Virginia Assembly repealed all penalties imposed on white servants for plundering during the revolt, but did not extend this pardon to black freemen and black indentured servants. Moreover, the gentry reinforced the separate labor status for each group: blacks were forced to occupy a racially subordinate and stigmatized status, one below all whites regardless of their class. Black was made to signify slave. In 1691, the assembly prohibited the manumission (freeing) of slaves unless the master paid for transporting them out of the colony. New laws sharpened the lines of a caste system: who was "black" was given expanded definition.[25]

With the creation of laws and social practices the elite created the social construct of race and the practice of racism. This is the reason why Dr. Tatum defined racism as prejudice plus power.[26] Consequently, blacks and other people of color have been fighting for centuries to be treated as people and not some derivative of property.

Pause: What did you learn in your history classes?

---

[24] Ibid., 64.
[25] Ibid., 67.
[26] Tatum, *"Why Are All the Black Kids Sitting Together in the Cafeteria?"*, 7.

Today, our current social system is predicated on those past laws and practices. A lot has changed since then but the position of blacks hasn't changed much. "More than 50 years ago, Congress enacted the most comprehensive antidiscrimination legislation in history, the Civil Rights Act of 1964. Half a century later in 2015, the same gaps in racial inequality remain or have grown deeper."[27] In July, 2016 an United Nations (U.N.) official for human rights, Attorney Maini Kiai traveled to United States to investigate rights on the freedom to assemble.[28] Mr. Kiai interviewed hundreds of people including protestors, police officers and community leaders. In his statement, he writes about the complex history of the United States and how this history includes stolen land from Native Americans and an economy based on slavery, which has caused Blacks to have issues with law enforcement, finding jobs, housing and funding for education. Mr. Kiai acknowledges that protesters have reasons to be angry. He writes, "There is justifiable and palpable anger in the black community over these injustices."[29] Therefore, these injustices keep Blacks and other people of color at a lower

---

[27] Angela Onwuachi-Willig, "Race and Racial Identity Are Social Constructs," *New York Times,* September 6, 2016, accessed January 6, 2017, http://www.nytimes/roomfordebates /2015/06/how-fluid-is-racial-identity/race-and-racial-identity-are-social-constructs.
[28] Max Bearak, "Sometimes it Takes an Outsider to Crystallize American's Enduring Racism," *The Washington Post,* August 1, 2016, accessed August 1, 2016, http://www.washingtonpost.com/news/worldviews/wp/2016/08/01/sometimes-it-takes-an-outsider-to-crystallize-enduring-racism/
[29] Ibid.

socioeconomic position than whites. This is what #BlackLivesMatter is fighting to change.

The #BlackLivesMatter movement was started by three queer black women Alicia Garza, Opal Tometi and Patrisse Cullors.[30] It was in response to the death of Trayvon Martin, an unarmed black teenager gunned down by George Zimmerman a biracial man. Mr. Zimmerman was the armed aggressor but was not convicted of any charges. The hashtag #BlackLivesMatter was created as an outcry on social media and then turned into a social movement.[31] The movement picked up steam and became a part of the national discussion after the deaths of two African American males, Michael Brown and Eric Garner. Both men were killed by police officers. The year was 2014 and more and more deaths of black and brown people were being reported across the nation. And, many of these reported killings were done by the hands of police officers.

Policing

For our purposes, I'll focus on the killing of black and brown people by police officers, a major occurrence across the country. Do these horrific incidents have anything to do with power? By now you would know the answer to be, "Yes." In recent years, the deaths of black

---

[30] "Herstory," *Black Lives Matter*, accessed June 3, 2016, http://www.blacklivesmatter.com/herstory/
[31] Ibid.

men and women by police officials have been covered throughout the social media and mainstream media. People like Michael Brown, Eric Garner, Sandra Bland, Tamir Rice and Freddie Gray Jr., to name a few, were taken from their loved ones by the hands of those who are supposed to protect and serve them. The pattern of these deaths, happening across the country, must be analyzed.

We first have to know the history of law enforcement and then I will cover recent events. Policing and police departments can be traced back to London, England during the early 1800s.[32] Early forms of policing in the American colonies were called watchmen. These were often men who volunteered to monitor their communities throughout the day and night. In addition to making sure their communities were safe they assisted with putting out fires, rebuilding homes and doing other community tasks. As the population grew and became more diverse, a formal style of policing started being implemented throughout United States. The typical reasons we are told for the building of formal policing and police departments was to reduce crime and serve law abiding citizens. This is true, but not the whole story.

As early as the 1700s American colonists, particularly in the cities of the North, began to see their population change and increase. People from Italy, Germany, Ireland and other European countries started coming to colonial

---

[32] Robert McNamara and Ronald Burns, *Multiculturalism in the Criminal Justice System* (Boston: McGraw Hill, 2009), 224.

America. Social tensions rose and riots broke out.[33] The social elites with economic and political capital established police departments to control the immigrant populations and racial minorities, and to protect their investments. These police departments were also used to maintain and continue the social standings of these elites.[34]

Policing in the south had a different but similar story. Early policing in the South took form of slave patrols. They were used "to prevent slave revolts and apprehend runaway slaves."[35] They were also used to watch over and intimidate slaves. Such tactics protected the property and investments of plantation owners, who were the social elites. Slave patrols were "considered by some experts as the first American police departments and were established as early as the 1740s. By 1750, every Southern colony maintained a slave patrol."[36] In order for plantation owners to maintain their control over the large slave population they created legislation called the Black Codes which were used to govern slaves. The slave patrollers enforced these codes.

These slave patrollers were mostly poor whites. Wealthy whites had the means to pay the fines that allowed them to opt out of being patrollers. Slave patrols were used to maintain and continue the social standings of

---

[33] Carol A. Archbold, *Policing A Text/Reader* (Los Angeles: Sage Publications, 2013), 4.
[34] Ibid., 227.
[35] Ibid., 226.
[36] Ibid.

the elites. This meant elites would stay at the top of society while immigrants, blacks and the poor would remain at the bottom. Also in the western colonies, the predecessors of our current police officers harassed and controlled the physical movement and social mobility of Chinese immigrants.

Policing has changed a lot from its beginnings but the surveillance, intimidation, harassment and social control of minorities has been a constant theme throughout the centuries. Law professor and scholar Karla McKanders, who I've aided in her research, has made strong comparisons between the functions of slave patrols of the past and current law enforcement officers who have been stopping and apprehending random Latino/as for deportation.[37] This further supports other researchers and scholars who have found that racial profiling continues to be a problem across the country. Michelle Alexander the author of *The New Jim Crow* shared how social elites in government and the private sector have aided and funded police departments around the country to overwhelmingly arrest and incarcerate Black and Latino men.[38] In her book Black Stats African Americans by the Numbers in the Twenty-First Century, Monique Morris writes, "67% of

---

[37] Karla Mari McKanders, "Immigration Enforcement and the Fugitive Slave Acts: Exploring Their Similarities," Catholic University Law Review 61, no. 4 (2012): 947-948, http://scholarship.law.edu.cgi/viewcontent.cgi?article=1032&context=lawrevi ew (accessed February 6, 2017).
[38] Michelle Alexander, *The New Jim Crow Mass Incarceration in the Age of Colorblindness* (New York: The New Press, 2012), 73.

Black Americans report that there is police brutality practiced in the area where they live, compared with 25% of white Americans."[39] She also found, "black motorists are nearly twice as likely to be arrested and nearly three times as likely as white motorists to experience force during interactions with law enforcement."[40]

Pause: This is deep. I need to breathe…

The Break Down

Thus far, we have learned that the elites constructed race to maintain their position. With the construction of race came a slew of laws and social systems to oppress people of color. To analyze the power moves of the elites and law enforcement we must identify their interests. In the remaining pages of this chapter I'll identify and focus on one main interest of the elites and law enforcement. I will then show how this interest is conveyed through the three dimensions of power.

The main interest of the elite is to maintain the social hierarchy that keeps them on top. They place this interest over anything and anybody. We see this throughout history and today. Minorities have been fighting for the end of discrimination but because of institutional discrimination many of our organizations and different

---

[39] Monique W. Morris, *Black Stats African American by the Numbers in the Twenty-First Century* (New York: The New Press, 2014), 62.
[40] Ibid., 63.

parts of our government continue to employ inequitable practices. This is the first dimension of power: issue. The second dimension, agenda, is the elite creating a biased system to control for anything that would threaten their interest and to do so, creating the police force.

> "The police institution is created by the emerging dominant class as an instrument for the preservation of its control over restricted access to basic resources, over the political apparatus governing this access, and over the labor force necessary to provide the surplus upon which the dominant class lives."[41]

This also provides an additional explanation as to why so few police officers are indicted and charged for killing black and brown people. Their actions are in line of what the elites wants.

The final dimension, manipulation, was set in play during the civil rights movement. "The rhetoric of 'law and order' was first mobilized in the late 1950s as southern governors and law enforcement officials attempted to generate and mobilize white opposition to the Civil Rights Movement."[42] From the presidency of Richard Nixon until

---

[41] Phillip L. Reichel, "Southern Slave Patrols as a Transitional Police Type," American Journal of Police 7, no. 2 (1988): 70,
http://www.heinonline.org/HOL/Page?handle=hein.journals/ajpol7&div=18&g_sent=1&collection=journals (accessed February 6, 2017).
[42] Alexander, The New Jim Crow Mass Incarceration in the Age of Colorblindness, 40.

now the rhetoric of law and order, get tough on crime, three strikes you're out and the mobilization of the war on drugs was used to overwhelmingly target and incarcerate black and brown men. And the incarceration of black and brown women has recently been on the rise. Although whites tend to use more drugs than blacks, blacks are disproportionately shown in the media using and selling drugs.[43] Crime became racialized and as a country we believed blacks were more prone to commit crime than whites, and we still do. Even minority communities believed this and supported tougher laws on crime, which were directed to people that looked like them. This falls in the third dimension of power, manipulation, as the control of black and brown bodies is critical to maintain the social hierarchy, which keeps white elites in power

The elites set the back drop and police departments are doing the heavy lifting. For police departments one of their main interests is to sustain their credibility in their communities. This is achieved through the authorization they get from the law and their professional standing in the community.[44]

Since the first police departments, policing has gone through three different eras in which they have

[43] Sakl Knafo, "When it Come to Illegal Drug Use, White America Does the Crime, Black America Gets the Time," *Huffington Post,* September 17, 2013, accessed January 30, 2017, http://www.huffingtonpost.com/2013/09/17/racial-disparity-drug-use_n_3941346.html.
[44] U.S. Department of Justice, *The Evolving Strategy of Policing*, 4th ed. National Institute of Justice, (Washington, DC), 1988.

approached their work. Currently, in the third era, police departments depend on community members to help with safety and crime prevention. This is hard to do if the community doesn't respect their local law enforcement. Law professor Adam Benforado the author of *Unfair the New Science of Criminal Injustice* has written that people are less likely to follow laws that seem unfair and/or unfairly enforced.[45] So, police departments will go to great lengths to preserve their professionalism and credibility. This interest is placed over the interest of the victims who have experienced police brutality. It's also placed over the victims' families who want to know the truth and details of what took place. We saw this happen in the case of Michael Brown and Sandra Bland. In Michael Brown's case, it was first reported by the St. Louis County Police Department that Brown physically assaulted an officer and shots were fired.[46] This is contrary to what witnesses reported and what the autopsy uncovered. Brown was shot a minimum of 6 times from distance and witnesses did not report seeing a struggle.[47] The Texas trooper reported, in Sandra Bland's case that "he removed Ms. Bland from her car to more safely conduct a traffic investigation."[48] A grand jury found his statements to be

---

[45] Adam Benforado, *Unfair The New Science of Criminal Justice* (New York: Crown Publishers, 2015), 229-230.
[46] Emily Brown, "Timeline Michael Brown shooting in Ferguson Mo.," *USA TODAY,* August 10, 2015, accessed June 3, 2016,
http://www.usatoday.com/story/news/nation/2014/08/14/michael-brown-ferguson-missouri-timeline/14051827/.
[47] Ibid.
[48] David Montgomery, "Texas Trooper Who Arrested Sandra Bland is Charged With Perjury," *The New York Times,* January 6, 2016, accessed June 3, 2016,

false because the police dashboard camera showed the officer forcibly removed her and threaten to taser Ms. Bland. This is all because she would not put out her cigarette.[49] These are representations of the first dimension of power, issue. These officers and their departments placed their interest over telling the truth. They wanted the public to believe that they were doing their job in a suitable manner.

These cases including the death of Freddie Gray in Baltimore were also examples of the second dimension, agenda. Police departments, local governments and local prosecutors around the country control the information and the evidence of all cases. Police departments also control the information regarding interactions they have with citizens and community members. They have access to all of the evidence and depending on the laws they decide what and when evidence will be shared. Freddie Gray was arrested by police and that same day he was admitted to the hospital. He had two surgeries and laid in a comma and Baltimore Police, "declined to comment on why he was arrested or how he was hurt."[50] A week after his arrest Mr. Gray died in the hospital. William "Billy" Murphy Jr., an attorney for the Gray family said, "Gary

http://www.nytimes.com/2016/01/07/us/texas-grand-jury-sandra-bland.html?_r=1.

[49] Ibid.

[50] Colin Campbell, "Man injured in Gilmor Homes arrest has spine surgery remains in coma," *The Baltimore Sun,* April 15, 2015, accessed June 3, 2016, http://www.baltimoresun.com/news/maryland/crime/bs-md-ci-gilmor-homes-arrest-folo-20150415-story.html.

lapsed into a coma, died, was resuscitated, stayed in a coma and on Monday, underwent extensive surgery at Shock Trauma. 'He clung to life for seven days,' he said."[51] The Baltimore Sun a local newspaper in Baltimore continued with:

> The attorney also said that the city has a camera above where the arrest occurred and requested that the footage be released to the public. "We believe the police are keeping the circumstances of Freddie's death secret until they develop a version of events that will absolve them of all responsibility," Murphy said. "However, his family and the citizens of Baltimore deserve to know the real truth; and will not stop until we get justice from Freddie."[52]

Sadly, it doesn't stop there. We know that in Lukes' three dimensions of power, issue, agenda and manipulation that manipulation includes the first two but also modifies the beliefs and desires of the affected people. To maintain their professionalism and credibility similar police departments and policing agencies will find ways to blame the victims for their own deaths. They will

[51] Natalie Sherman, Chris Kaltenbach and Colin Campbell, "Freddie Gray dies a week after being injured during arrest," *The Baltimore Sun,* April 19, 2015, accessed June 3, 2016,
http://www.baltimoresun.com/news/maryland/freddie-gray/bs-md-freddie-gray-20150419-story.html#page=1.
[52] Ibid.

discredit the victim's character, question the victim's health and/or play out the stereotypes that were assigned to the victim's race. Some of these tactics were used against Mr. Gray.

Mr. Eric Garner a black male was arrested by police on Thursday, July 17, 2014 in New York City.[53] During his arrest an officer used an illegal chokehold to take Mr. Garner down to the ground. Garner kept saying he couldn't breathe and went into cardiac arrest. He was pronounced dead later that day. The autopsy showed that Garner died because of the chokehold but the Patrolmen's Benevolent Association, a union that represents officers in the NYPD alluded to the fact that it was Garner's behavior that led to his interaction with the police and his health and weight contributed to his own death.[54]

Twelve-year-old Tamir Rice, who was playing with a toy pellet gun was gunned down by police within seconds of police arrival. The Cuyahoga County Prosecutor's Office asked for outside reviews to determine if the officer was justified for using deadly force so quickly. The outside reviewers who were former law enforcement said the officer was justified because he did not know if the gun was a fake.[55] However, a Municipal Court judge, "in

[53] NBC York, "Timeline Eric Garner Death," *NBC New York,* December 3, 2014, accessed June 6, 2016,
http://www.nbcnewyork.com/news/local/Timeline-Eric-Garner-Chokehold-Death-Arrest-NYPD-Grand-Jury-No-Indictment-284657081.html.
[54] Ibid.
[55] Chicago Tribune, "Officer's Shooting of Tamir Rice Justified, 2 Outside Reports Rule," *Chicago Tribune*, October 11, 2015, accessed June 6, 2016,

Cleveland, Ohio determined that probable cause exists to bring murder charges" against the officer and he could face "involuntary manslaughter, reckless homicide, negligent homicide and dereliction of duty."[56] However, mainstream society still plays into the narrative of blaming the victims. Within our collective consciousness, we justify the police's actions and believe that somehow these people deserved to die. You see these types of reactions and statements all over social media. People of all backgrounds defend the actions of the police who were fundamentally designed to control minorities. Maintaining such thoughts and ideas as a society is against our own interests. This is what makes the third dimension of power, manipulation, so toxic.

The police are a part of a system to maintain the status quo. The harassment and killing of racial and ethnic minorities by police officers isn't a bad thing in the context of our system. They are doing what the system wants. This is a hard truth to accept and it's an easier one to deny. To deny the truth is to deny our full capacity to change the current system and to make our reality more just. I have no issues with individual police officers or with whites for that matter. But I do have a deep problem with a system that was designed to control black and

http://www.chicagotribune.com/news/nationworld/ct-tamir-rice-shooting-20151010-story.html.
[56] Ian Millhiser, "Breaking Judge Says Cause Exists to Arrest Cop Who Killed Tamir Rice for Murder," *Think Progress*, June 11, 2015, accessed June 6, 2016, http://www.thinkprogress.org/justice/2015/06/11/3668877/breaking-judge-says-cause-exists-arrest-cop-kill-tamir-rice-murder/.

brown bodies. This system is so corrosive that researchers Vicky Wilkins and Brian Williams found that even minority police officers tend to turn a blind eye or they themselves have participated in racial profiling of people who look like them.[57] We have criminalized race and acted out rituals of punishment against racial and ethnic minorities that can only be described as an awful form of "human sacrifice."[58]

Yea, like Rick Ross said it this is, "deeper than rap."[59] And it ain't so far-fetched when T.I. said "we livin' in a warzone."[60]

Pause: Thoughts?

---

[57] Vicky M. Wilkins and Brian N. Williams, "Black or Blue: Racial Profiling and Representative Bureaucracy," American Society for Public Administration, 68, no. 4 (2008): 657, http://www.jstor.org/stable/25145649 (accessed April 5, 2016).

[58] Alexander, The New Jim Crow Mass Incarceration in the Age of Colorblindness, 170.

[59] Rick Ross, "Deeper Than Rap," Genius, http://www.genius.com/albums/Rick-ross/Deeper-than-rap.

[60] T.I., "Warzone," Azlyrics, http://www.azlyrics.com/lyrics/ti/warzone.html.

Chapter Three

Potential Control

A person one day asked me, "Colber, where can you find the most human potential?" When I said, "Where?" He replied, "The grave yard." This question and answer has stuck with me over the years. To think that so many people died with their full potential untapped. We will never know their full beauty and our world will never benefit from their full inner source. However, this tragedy happens every day. People go through life failing to become the best versions of themselves. Who is to blame for this travesty? Is the person to blame? Are their family and friends to blame? Is society to blame? But before we can answer these questions we must ask ourselves, "What is potential and does everyone have it?"

In my experience, human potential can be very subjective. People define potential in regards to their world views and perceptions. I have also seen potential defined by a person's culture and economic class. I think all of these definitions can be true. However, for our purposes we need specifics. In Webster's New World College Dictionary, the second definition states potential is something, "that can, but has not yet, come into being; possible; latent; unrealized; underdeveloped."[61] I like this definition because it has less of a deficient tone and more

---

[61] Michael Agnes, ed., *Webster's New World College Dictionary* (Cleveland: Wiley Publishing Inc, 2004), 1126.

of a tone of possibility. This tone of possibility is well recorded during the human potential movement.

The human potential movement is a relatively new concept in human history. It can be traced back to the 1950's when middle class people were wanting more out of life.[62] One of the leaders of this movement was the psychologist Abraham Maslow. Professor Maslow is best known for his hierarchy of needs theory which explains that people have different motivations that dictate their behavior and aspirations. The theory's premise is that people have innate motivations that push them to be their best selves or in other words there is something inside ALL of us that pushes us to want reach our potential.

I bring up this well-known theory that is used in multiple disciplines because it explains human potential in practical ways. I will use it to explain how to develop potential. It is also a theory that lends itself to be coupled with other theories. So, I will couple Maslow's hierarchy of needs and Lukes' power dimensions to show how those in power can control and stifle the potential of those with less power. We have learned Lukes' power dimensions and now let's learn Maslow's theory.

Maslow begins by explaining, "the starting point for motivation theory are the so-called physiological needs,"

---

[62] Debra Ollivier, "The Esalen Institute and The Human Potential Movement Turn 50," *The Huffington Post,* July 24, 2012, accessed March 28, 2016, http://www.huffingtonpost.com/debra-olliver/the-esalen-institute-and-the-human-potential-movement-turns-50_b_1536989.html.

the physical needs for survival.[63] As living organisms our bodies automatically maintain the constant circulation of blood. Maslow referred to this as homeostasis. In order for the body to continue doing this job well our bodies need food, water, protein, salt, sugar, oxygen, vitamins, etc. to function. Other physiological conditions and/or basic needs are fatigue, sleepiness, maternal behavior, sex, activity and exercise. These basic physiological needs, the first level of the hierarchy, motivate us to acquire and maintain them to stay alive. Therefore, they are the most important needs to a human being. Now each level in this hierarchy explains the motivations and behavior of an individual and the steps it takes for someone to reach their full potential.

The second level to this hierarchy is safety. The safety needs include, "security; stability; dependency; protection; freedom from fear, from anxiety and chaos; need for structure, order, law, limits; strength in the protector; and so on."[64] As you can see from this list people need to feel safe mentally and physically. Maslow suggests that the role of education is to neutralize the world's "dangers through knowledge", so to ease the mind of the individual.[65] From a physical stand point a healthy adult lives in a secure society where ordinarily members "feel safe enough from" extreme temperatures, wild

---

[63] Abraham Maslow, *Motivation and Personality* (New York: Harper & Row, Publishers, 1954), 35.
[64] Ibid., 39.
[65] Ibid.

animals, chaos, tyranny, criminal assault, murder and so on.[66] For an adult to feel safe physically and emotionally she/he/ze needs to be able to get a job, and have job security in order to afford to save, obtain health insurance and social security in their old age.

Once the basic and safety needs of a person are sufficiently gratified the next needs in the hierarchy include belongingness and love. This level explains that a person seeks love and affection from others. She would hunger to belong in groups and to find a place among her communities. She would want to know her roots and her groups' roots and origins. Finally, "not to be overlooked is the fact that the love needs involve both giving and receiving love."[67]

The next phase of the hierarchy of needs is esteem. "All people in our society have a need or desire for a stable, firmly based, usually high evaluation of themselves, for self-respect, or self-esteem, and for the esteem of others."[68] The esteem need is broken into two sub categories. The first point deals with the person internally. A person seeks internal strength, achievement and adequacy. She/he/ze will seek mastery, competence and confidence to face the world while wanting independence and freedom. The second point deals with the external. She is desiring respect, prestige, attention,

---

[66] Ibid., 41.
[67] Ibid., 45.
[68] Ibid.

recognition, dignity and or appreciation from others. Healthy self-esteem and recognition is based on deserved respect and not, "external fame or celebrity and unwarranted adulation."[69]

The final phase and the peak of the pyramid is the need for self-actualization, this "refers to man's desire for self-fulfillment, namely, to the tendency for him to become actualized in what he is potentially."[70] At this level individuals have a desire to become who they are naturally and do the things that come naturally to them. Within that individuals desire to be their best version and accepting their full selves. These people accept the world for what it truly is and take actions to make it a better place. Again, we must remember that in order for people to explore or even desire this need they must have satisfied all their prior needs. The next page has a depiction of the model.[71]

---

[69] Ibid., 46.
[70] Ibid.
[71] Saul McLeod, "Maslow's Hierarchy of Needs," *SimplyPsychology,* http://www.simplypsychology.org/maslow.html.

Before we move forward I must add this point. There are some researchers like Dr. Mark Koltko-Rivera who argue that before Maslow's death, he discovered a more final need than self-actualization called self-transcendence. A person who desires self-transcendence is seeking "to further a cause beyond the self and to experience a communion beyond the boundaries of the self through peak experience."[72] This means a person no longer focuses on self but on something external like truth, justice and/or enlightenment. They transcend personal needs to have peak experiences with the external world. An argument such as this is noted for our discussion but must be explored at another time, in another book.

Pause: Where are you in Maslow's
Hierarchy of Needs?

---

[72] Mark E. Koltko-Rivera, "Rediscovering the Later Version of Maslow's Hierarchy of Needs: Self-Transcendence and Opportunities for Theory, Research, and Unification," Review of General Psychology 10, no. 4 (2006): 303, http://www.pages.stolaf.edu/psych-391-spring15/files/2014/02/Koltko-RIvera.pdf (accessed August 8, 2015).

Now, according to Maslow we have tools within us to reach each level of the hierarchy. Our cognitive capacities like our intellect, our ability to learn and other functions are the "adjustive tools" that we implement to satisfy our basic needs.[73] If these tools are in danger then the natural curiosity of people for the search of truth, knowledge and wisdom is stifled by censorship, secrecy, dishonesty and the blocking of communication and threaten people from achieving their basic needs.[74]

Consequently, I argue if someone, an institution, social system or country, has the means or the power to block people's cognitive capacities or only allows people to meet certain needs, then such powers can decide who is allowed to explore and/or reach their potential. Therefore, the potential of those with less power can be influenced and/or controlled by those with more power. This argument is the crux of this book. It is the main point!

This same idea was noted by Maslow. In a Maslow biography, author Edward Hoffman wrote that Maslow was interested in the Civil Rights movement and the progress of Black people. During one of his visits to Boston University, in the 1960's, Maslow told students that in order for Black Americans to reach their full potential they must overcome socioeconomic discrimination, failing public schools, etc.[75] Socioeconomic discrimination in this

---

[73] Maslow, *Motivation and Personality*, 47.
[74] Ibid.
[75] Edward Hoffman, *The Right to be Human A Biography of Abraham Maslow* (New York: Jeremy P. Teacher INC., 1988), 311.

context includes the practices of racism and classism, which are forms of power that allow those in power and/or the institutions of power to control and/or influence the potential of individuals. Let me show you how this plays out in real life and in different situations.

To do so, in the following section I will use Maslow's hierarchy and Lukes' dimensions of power to show how power can control human potential. And, I will begin with the basic needs and end on the needs of self-actualization. For each need I will use a different marginalized group to show how the powers of the dominant group have kept certain people disenfranchised and/or oppressed.

Power vs. Potential

Let's start with power controlling our basic needs. A prime example is the Flint, Michigan water crisis. What we know is that water is one of our basic needs. In 2015, people around North America, and the world, started hearing about how the water in Flint, Michigan was not safe to consume. Then in February, 2016 TIME Magazine released an issue that focused on Flint.[76]

The magazine reported that in 2011, the city of Flint was facing $15 million in debt due to the declining economy. Governor Rick Snyder appointed four emergency managers to run the city to save money. The interest of Governor Snyder and the city managers was to

---

[76] Josh Sanbrun, "The Toxic Tap," *Time Magazine,* February 1, 2016, 32.

save money. Their idea was to stop buying water from Detroit because the cost of buying water from Detroit almost doubled between 2004 and 2013. To replace this water supply from Detroit, Flint would get its water from nearby Lake Huron by creating a new water pipeline. Karegnondi Water Authority (KWA) was to lead this project. The expectation was that these changes would save Flint $19 million dollars over eight years. However, two problems came up. The pipeline to Lake Huron wouldn't be built until 2016 and Detroit would stop selling water to Flint by April 2014. So, in the meantime, between time, the few in charge decided to get water from the Flint River, and they didn't tell the public. They also did not hold a city-council vote. These actions describe the first and second dimensions of Lukes' power theory, when the few placed their interests over the Flint citizens and protected themselves by excluding anybody or anything that could hurt them. *TIME Magazine* reported that the Flint leaders were excited about this decision because of "their fiscal prudence."[77]

The switch was made but it turned out that the Flint River had high levels of chloride and was not treated with a corrosion inhibitor. As the water passed through the city's old lead pipes it absorbed the lead from the pipes. Within four months the city found E. coli in the water and told residents to boil their water before consuming it. The citizens of Flint started calling and filing complaints about

---

[77] Ibid., 36.

the water. Doctors in Flint were seeing a rise in hair loss, rashes and other ailments. But local leaders were ignoring the people and kept saying the water was safe and there were only isolated problems. However, doctors found that a large percentage of children were suffering from lead poisoning after environmentalists discovered high levels of lead in the water.

Then local citizens with the help of researchers were able to get the water switched back to Detroit water on October 16, 2015. Flint leaders did try to employ their power the way Lukes described in the third dimension. They kept telling people the water was fine even though it was against the people's own welfare and they tried to discredit an employee of U.S. Environmental Protection Agency, who wrote a memo about the water crisis prior to everything hitting the fan. But the people weren't having it!

Looking at this situation from a Maslow perspective, those in the position of power in the city and state governments were blocking the people from getting their basic needs. People were using their cognitive capacities to figure out how to get access to clean water for themselves and their families. According to Maslow's theory, the citizens of Flint could not achieve self-actualization because they were consumed with getting clean water. But that's not all. Because of the lead poisoning the children of Flint may experience development issues which may affect their cognitive capacities. If that's not sad enough there's evidence that show communities with large minority populations across the country have experienced environmental issues and pollution caused by chemical waste companies, mining and landfills.[78] We need more people talking about and working for environmental justice. Polluting the water, air or other natural resources will directly impact people's most basic needs. If we can't get clean water and healthy food, then our potential is very much limited.

Safety Needs

As we know the next step in the hierarchy of needs is safety. An issue dat mainstream media does not cover thoroughly are the safety needs of undocumented immigrants. Being that most of my family members are from outside of the United States I have witnessed the fear of deportation and how it can consume people's lives. Contrary to popular belief, undocumented people have done great things in the United States. However, this good may not increase because their potential is stifled by fear.

Researchers, Margaret Sullivan and Roberta Rehm, found that undocumented Mexican immigrants (UMIs) face a number of mental and physical health issues. UMIs

---

[78] Regina Austin and Michael Schill, "Black, Brown, Poor & Poisoned: Minority Grassroots Environmentalism and the Quest for Eco-Justice," The Kansas Journal of Law & Public Policy, 69 (1991): 69-70, http://www.scholarship.law.upenn.edu/cgi/viewcontent.cgi?article=1808&context=faculty_scholarship (accessed November 3, 2015).

are at risk of eroded self-worth, low self-esteem, depression, guilt and shame.[79] They do not seek healthcare because of the fear of being detected. Sullivan and Rehm write that the, "intensity and pervasiveness of fear in the lives of UMIs is nearly ubiquitous in the literature. Fear of detection and deportation is constant, regardless of length of time in the United States."[80] They continue by stating the, "experience of fear becomes integrated into daily life and shapes the perception of reality, leading to "habitual fear reactions."[81] Thus, fear is a barrier to receiving healthcare when patient-provider trust is eroded because of the need for secrecy."[82] A study published by the United States' National Institutes of Health (NIH) claims, "it is reasonable to expect that long-term exposure to stress associated with fear of deportation is likely to have a negative impact on an individual's thoughts, emotions, and social functioning."[83] They also found that deportation has increased more than fivefold between 1996-2008.[84] Latino/as reported in a national survey in 2008, that questioning from law enforcement of their legal status increased and there has been more "workplace raids by

---

[79] Margaret M. Sullivan and Roberta Rehm, "Mental Health of Undocumented Mexican Immigrants," Advances in Nursing Science 28, no. 3 (2005): 248, http://www.williamperezphd.com/articles/sullivan-rehm-2005.pdf (accessed June 9, 2016).
[80] Ibid.
[81] Ibid.
[82] Ibid.
[83] Consuelo Arbona, Norma Olvera, Nestor Rodriguez, Jacqueline Hagan, Adriana Linares and Margit Wiesner, "Acculturative Stress Among Documented and Undocumented Latino Immigrants in the United States," Hispanic Journal of Behavioral Sciences 32, no. 3 (2010): 379, doi 10.1177/0739986310373210.
[84] Ibid.

government agents. Stricter enforcement of the immigration laws and higher deportation rates of Latino immigrants have resulted in higher levels of family separation, fear, and stress among Latinos, particular undocumented immigrants."[85] Immigration is a complex issue in the United States and we needed immigration reform years ago. Side note, don't get me started on states like Arizona who are racially profiling and discriminating against their Latino/a residents.

In the previous chapter, I wrote about the United States' history of controlling people of color through laws and law enforcement. The interest of many local governments and parts of the federal government, specifically Congress, is to displace immigrants. This interest is placed over the health and welfare of immigrants, their families and the larger community. The brutality of displacement is revealed through the unfair immigration laws and their enforcement. Their power is taken to Lukes' second dimension by creating a culture of fear that limits undocumented immigrants to reach out to government agencies and to participate in the political process. These effects place this situation in the third dimension of power, manipulation. NIH found that because of the fear of deportation documented and undocumented Latino/as are less likely to, "walk in the streets, ask for help from government agencies, report an infraction to the police, report to the police an infraction

---

[85] Ibid.

committed against one's person, attend court if requested to do so, apply for a driver's license, and wait in the street corner to get work."[86] Not taking part of these activities does not benefit Latino/as or other immigrant populations but those in power.

Belongingness and Love Needs

I spend a significant amount of time working with adolescents and traditional aged college students (18-25) around topics of leadership, diversity, masculinity and substance abuse prevention. Some of my most emotional experiences working with young adults came from my time as a college administrator. Diverse student groups would come to my office and share with me how they have been rejected by different people and/or organizations that they came in contact with. A group of young people I'd like to mention here are those who identify on the LGBTQ+ (Lesbian, Gay, Bisexual, Transgender, Queer) continuum.

Once safety needs are gratified a person will hunger for affection, acceptance and love. This is Maslow's third group of needs. However, large groups of people are denied these needs due to hatred and discrimination. For example, people who are LGBTQ+ encounter homophobia, the practice of discrimination against those who are not heterosexual. They have been discriminated

---

[86] Ibid., 369.

against and/or killed around the world. I would venture to say there also exists discrimination against people who neither seem to be heterosexual or express themselves in the traditional gender roles of a man or woman.

Adolescents who are LGBTQ+ have to live with the fact that they will be rejected by society and more sadly by their family and friends. Research has found that adolescents who are sexual minorities do not do well with rejection from their family, friends and communities. This rejection leads to severe consequences for young people who are developing psychologically and emotionally. Thirty years of research suggests that adolescents who are sexual minorities struggle with, "higher rates of depressive symptoms, suicidal ideation, and suicide attempts than their heterosexual peers."[87] Research has also documented that they are at higher risk of abusing alcohol, using illicit drugs and taking part of other risky behaviors.[88] They are also at a higher risk for being homeless.[89] Such rejection works contrary to Maslow's

---

[87] Gary M. Diamond, Guy Shilo, Erin Jurgensen, Anthony D'Augelli, Valeria Samarova and Khendi White, "How Depressed and Suicidal Sexual Minority Adolescents Understand the Causes of Their Distress," Journal of Gay & Lesbian Mental Health 15, no. 2 (2011): 131, doi 10.1080/19359705.2010.532668.

[88] Tonda L. Hughes and Michele Eliason, "Substance Use and Abuse in Lesbian, Gay, Bisexual and Transgender Populations," The Journal of Primary Prevention 22, no. 3 (2002): 289-290, doi 10.1023/A:1013669705086.

[89] Caitlin Ryan, Stephen T. Russell, David Huebner, Rafael Diaz and Jorge Sanchez, "Family Acceptance in Adolescence and the Health of LGBT Young Adults" Journal of Child and Adolescent Psychiatric Nursing 23, no. 4 (2010): 206, doi 10.1111/j.1744-6171.2010.00246.x.

hierarchy of needs, which makes it harder for young people to reach their potential.

Homophobia as a power structure dehumanizes and rejects LGBTQ+ people. It puts the interests of heterosexual people first and it informs our social and political structures to keep LGBTQ+ people out. Finally, homophobia causes people to hurt themselves because they are not considered "normal." Homophobia covers all three dimensions of power: issue, agenda, and manipulation.

Pause: All of this is getting really heavy. Breathe…

Esteem Needs

To take it to the business sector, the Harvard Business Review published an article titled *Women and Minorities are Penalized for Promoting Diversity* by researchers Dr. Stefanie Johnson and Dr. David Hekman.[90] These researchers begin their article by stating roughly 85%, "of corporate executives and board members are white men".[91] This hasn't changed much for decades. This is because white men hire and promote other white men. So, the researchers wanted to see if women and minorities benefited from hiring people like themselves. In their

---

[90] Stefanie K. Johnson and David R. Hekman, "Women and Minorities are Penalized for Promoting Diversity" *Harvard Business Review,*
http://www.hbr.org/2016/03/women-and-minorities-are-penalized-for-promoting-diversity.
[91] Ibid.

study, they found that women and minorities executives who frequently engaged in promoting diversity and balance were, "rated much worse by their bosses."[92] For the black people that I know, this ain't new information. But now there's research to prove it. Johnson and Hekman also found that working adults rated female managers and nonwhite managers less effective when these mangers did not hire a white male. To explain these findings the researchers talked about the power gaps between men and women and between whites and no for other women and nonwhites, it highlights their low-status demographics, activating the stereotype of incompetence, and leads to worse performance ratings.[93]

Now, what we know about the esteem level in the hierarchy of needs is that being respected and recognized by others is one of the two sub categories. When women or ethnic/racial minorities are rated lower by their bosses because their bosses don't respect or value diversity, those people may be kept from fulfilling their esteem needs. Countless of studies have shown women and minorities not being fairly treated and/or undervalued in the workplace. Furthermore, there's research that proves diversity within organizations can increase innovation, which is important in the age of ideas. And if companies are not innovating they will most likely be out of business.

---

[92] Ibid.
[93] Ibid.

The work of Dr. Johnson and Dr. Hekman shows us that majority of businesses want to maintain the status quo and place their interest above women, minorities and an ever-increasing diverse reality. The corporate ladder is a system that doesn't reward or value those of diverse backgrounds nor encourage or promote diversity. This article demonstrates the first and the second dimensions of Lukes' theory.

Need for Self-Actualization

Maslow's final level is self-actualization. I'mma tell you the truth, I ain't even want to cover self-actualization because I think we ain't even there, yet as society. There's too much injustice! Examples include the ways we have treated and continue to treat Natives Americans and other indigenous people around the world and how we treat all people of color. Further examples include how we villainize people of the Muslim faith, discriminate against people who have a Middle Eastern background, victimize and blame rape survivors, mistreat people with disabilities, push aside people with mental health issues and the list goes on. BUT one of the many ways we can improve our society and world is by getting more people like you to reach out and maintain their full potential.

The motivations for people who have reached the pinnacle of Maslow's hierarchy of needs include, "character growth, character expression, maturation, and development."[94] Their need is to be their best selves. To achieve this goal, they employ their own code of ethics and hold themselves to a higher standard. They are both independent and dependent. Self-actualizing people are humble, creative, unique and they all have a purpose to better the world. These people are also able to love themselves and others more fully because they deeply understand and accept themselves. Maslow makes it clear that these people aren't perfect because nobody is perfect but these are the most psychologically healthy individuals.

I then thought about people in our society who have and/or are likely to reach self-actualization and two people come up. I reached out to my friends and the first person that came up was Michelle Obama. The other person that came to mind was Dr. Doris Ching. Dr. Ching isn't as famous as Michelle Obama but she has made waves in the field of higher education and administration. She has also been a champion for Asians college students and Asian administrators.

Finally, Maslow points out that we must support a democratic culture and society that produces many self-actualizing people. In fact, our society will benefit from them because they will be model citizens, as Maslow maintained. However, we aren't there and we have a lot of work to do. If we continue to ostracize and negatively use power to control people's potential, millions will never become self-actualizing people. They will be shut

---

94 Maslow, *Motivation and Personality*, 159.

out from their better selves. They will have #NoEntry to
their full potential.

Chapter Four

Thinking and Living Consciously

Without freedom of mind there can be no true and lasting freedom.[95]*- bell hooks*

Freedom! This is such a loaded word and it means so many things to so many people. When I was in graduate school, in the field of student affairs and college administration I came to realize that freedom for the students I worked with was giving them the space, knowledge, assistance and tools for them to become who they wanted to become. This meant giving them the freedom to explore their own identities and allowing them to make the choices of who they will be or how they will show up in different social spaces. I use this same idea here. Freedom in the context of this book is that you as a full human being have the power and right to control your environment to reach your full potential. However, we have learned from the previous chapters we all don't have this freedom. But we bout to change the game. This chapter and the next will provide ideas, information, solutions, strategies and tips for you and your village to achieve y'alls full and shared potential.

Pause: How do you define freedom?

---

[95] bell hooks, *Rock my Soul Black People and Self-Esteem* (New York: Atria Books, 2003), 93.

I believe in order for us to reach this freedom we must build our consciousness of ourselves and of this world. Consciousness can mean many things but I think of it like this; I no longer blindly believe what mainstream society tells me about me. And I will educate myself about myself to create my own ideas of myself. I will become conscious about me. When a person has a subordinate identity the story of that identity is already manufactured for that person to assume. She/he/ze is supposed to act accordingly within the parameters of that identity. Those parameters and the narrative of that specific identity were created by the dominant group. I also believe that dominant groups suffer for creating and maintaining such parameters for the subordinate. They have to operate within their own parameters and if they aren't intentional, their abilities to be conscious and engage with those different from them is severely impaired. Over and above, as a full human being you have the right to accept what people and society tells you about you and your identities. And if you rightfully choose that, I respect it. But if you chose it without doing your own self exploration and you stopped short of expanding your consciousness, did you really choose it? Don't get me wrong, I'm not asking you to change who you are. What I am asking you to do is to constantly explore and educate yourself about yourself. You owe that to yourself and everybody else.

I was eager to share other theories and philosophies from academics and activists like Paulo Freire, bell hooks and Terrell Strayhorn. But when I meditated about this chapter I realized I have learned things about myself and my own story when I heard other stories of perseverance. Those stories made my story even more relevant. So, in the remaining pages of this chapter I will share a story. I will share how I struggled with an identity and then came to love and accept it. My hope is that you can find some parallels from my story to your own. Most importantly, I hope you have the courage to acknowledge that your story is already great and that you can make it even greater!

Story Time

My formal education started in pre-school, which I don't remember much. But when I started elementary school I do remember struggling with the class material. I had issues with math, reading, writing and speaking. I didn't understand it. In my own mind, I knew I was smart and capable but I couldn't express it. This inability to express my mastery of the class material was so noticeable that I was constantly made fun of by my peers. They called me dumb and stupid and I remember crying a lot about school. I cried when other kids made fun of me, when I was frustrated with myself, and when I was struggling with school work. By far what hurt the most was that I was trying really hard.

As I got older and went to middle school I had a better sense of what I thought were short comings and I hid them from my peers and teachers. I over compensated with my personality and good behavior. But these compensations never remediated the problem of me thinking that I wasn't smart enough or good enough to be an above average student, even though I was still able to pass my classes and graduate from middle and high school with a B average. I was also good enough to get accepted to one of the top private colleges in the south.

When in college, the school work got realer! It took me so much more time to study and complete my work. In the spring semester of my sophomore year a professor and mentor, Ms. Paula McGhee suggested I should get tested on learning capabilities. She said she couldn't put her finger on it but she expressed something wasn't adding up when it came to my work in comparison to my ability to effectively express myself during class discussions. Side note, she also her class was great and very interesting. However, I was just too involved with campus activities. So, she suggested that I go to the learning center on campus.

I went there and after their assessment they arranged for me to meet with a psychologist. After several weeks working with the psychologist I found out that I was dyslexic and had learning disabilities or learning differences (LD). I also found out that I had an above average IQ. I had mix feelings about my results. I felt a sense of relief because I knew I was different but I couldn't express it because I didn't know what it was. With the test results, I thought I was deficient and felt embarrassed. The stereotypes of people with learning issues flooded my mind. I thought that they were not normal, that they couldn't handle the regular curriculum. They saw things backwards. And they were dumb. I felt those same emotions from my childhood. Nevertheless, after my results I started receiving accommodations for my classes. In addition to the accommodations, I received help from the learning center and I started implementing new study strategies that were tailored to my learning styles. As for my grades, I went from a B/C student to an A/B student just in one semester. I was amazed! My parents were too. I was getting it done.

I graduated college and while in graduate school I spent some time researching LD. My family and friends were so encouraging and would tell me LD was a gift. But I had a hard time believing them. I didn't just want to keep accepting the negative labels that were placed on people with LD. I didn't want to continue stereotyping myself and others like me. I had to figure out what LD meant for me, ya dig. So, for my different courses I wrote research papers that focused on learning disabilities. I was conducting my own research about one of my identities. I thank my professors for giving me the flexibility to write on the topics I was interested in. What I learned about LD gave me freedom. I had the freedom to learn the whole truth and to find my own truth. I learned that our education system wasn't and isn't designed to be inclusive of all types of learners. It was and still is designed to teach a certain type of learner. The research showed me that there are millions of people who have LD and our education system is failing them. I learned that people with LD are quite intelligent and they express their intelligence in different and creative ways. I learned that learning disabilities were considered to be invisible disabilities. This meant people couldn't tell if I was a person with LD by just looking at me or even by knowing me. At the time, I thought this was a good thing because I could hide my LD and pretend I was "normal." This was problematic on multiple levels. On the individual level I wasn't being true to myself which hindered me from fully loving and accepting me for me. Due to this type of invisibility, as a society we cannot have an ongoing conversation on how to make our world more inclusive for all types of learners. Inevitably, main stream society doesn't acknowledge the everyday existence of people with learning disabilities and uses shorthanded information like stereotypes to describe us.

During that process of exploration, I was reading a book about people with LD and in most of their stories they encouraged others with LD to share who they are and try to make the world a better place for all learners. I was really moved by this. So, much so that in one of my classes my final project was about students with dyslexia and LD in higher education. While presenting my final project, I told my peers that I was a person with dyslexia and LD. As I was sharing I felt tears coming because I didn't want them to make fun of me like back in elementary school. I held back my tears and watched their faces. When I shared this identity with them I wanted a round of applause but they just looked intently waiting for me to continue. It was an intense moment.

When I graduated with my Masters I started working a full-time position but I continued my research about my dyslexia and LD identity. I began to somewhat recognize the certain gifts that came with these identities. But they didn't really crystalize until I left that position. After some time working at an institution I transitioned to working on my own business.

In the first year of working on my business full time, I was reading and listening to Malcolm Gladwell's book *David and Goliath*. While reading this book, I learned that a large number of successful entrepreneurs were dyslexic.[96] And, Gladwell dedicated a whole chapter in his book about successful people with dyslexia. He found that because people with dyslexia were often ridiculed and struggled in school they developed perseverance, social risk taking and other skills. Some of the skills mentioned were listening, negotiating, posing and strategic planning.[97] This for me made so much sense and it helped me explain my own experience. I struggled in school because of my dyslexia and LD but I developed other skills and methods to be successful. When I thought of my consulting firm, I made sure I spent a lot of time listening to our clients and asking the right questions. This is part

---

[96] Malcolm Gladwell, *David and Goliath Underdogs, Misfits, and The Art of Battling Giants* (New York: Little, Brown and Company, 2013), 106.
[97] Ibid., 107-124.

of the reason why our clients are satisfied with our services. And because I had to strategically plan to pass my classes back in school, I've assisted my clients with their strategic plans. Furthermore, let's be real about it; this book and the way it's written is a social risk. But I've been taking social risks all my life. So, this comes natural.

To this day, I explore my dyslexic and LD identities. I am more open to sharing my identities and making the world a better place for all types of learners. It is with these perspectives I've been given opportunities to present about dyslexia and LD. Several years ago, I did a presentation with my colleague and brother, Joe Fitzgerald III at The Alumni of Color Conference (AOCC) held at the Harvard Graduate School of Education. Our presentation was about black males with LD. We shared our stories and how we can improve our educational system. We talked about what it meant to have those identities and how they intersect with our racial identity. The presentation went well and our surveys showed that the audience was satisfied. But most of all I was proud of myself because I came so far.

I came from being ashamed of who I was to vigorously trying to love my full self. I have to admit I don't always love myself everyday as much as I should but as each day passes I continue to free my mind of the negative label. Since learning about my dyslexia and LD I've gotten closer and closer to fully loving and accepting myself in all that I am. And that is enough for me right now.

We know in Maslow's hierarchy of needs that one must love themselves and accept themselves in order for them to achieve their full potential. If I wasn't thinking and living consciously I wouldn't have explored these identities about myself. I would have thought I wasn't smart enough and would have continued hiding myself from myself. And I may have not allowed myself the opportunity to present at Harvard University. But at the end of the day I wanted more for me. This isn't just about going to college, because our personal journeys look and feel different and that is fine. This isn't about Ivy League schools either. I believe it's about you finding you and you figuring out what you want for yourself. What I want for me is to be the best person I can be. That's my dream! But, if I allow others whose goals are to oppress me and to make me feel small what happens to my dreams? I think J Cole said it best, "even if you let em' kill your dream it'll haunt you."[98] It's tough to live a life being haunted by your dead dreams. So, do you and get to know you!

Pause: How do you love yourself more and how does loving yourself more connect to your dreams?

---

[98] J Cole, "A Tale of 2 Cities," Direct Lyrics, http://www.directlyrics.com/j-cole-a-tale-of-2-citiez-lyrics.html.

Chapter Five

Living Strategically = Power & Access

May the optimism of tomorrow be your foundation for today[99]-
Wale

The purpose of the chapter is to give you some general strategies in navigating a world with competing powers. These strategies have worked for me and the people around me. I will also be sharing more of my faith because I believe it has been a major factor in my success. I don't share my faith to convert anybody but as a means to share my full story.

We have learned that people and institutions don't always have our best interests in mind. This doesn't mean we give up. It means that we have to live life more strategically and to be very intentional in pursuing our dreams in the mist of other power players. I wish I could give you a playbook with a play by play to assist you with your actions and decisions regarding the external forces that are at opposition to your interests. However, life is too complicated and I haven't lived your life. Therefore, in this chapter I will provide you with some general strategies to navigate this world of supportive and opposing powers. I will share with you some things to keep in mind while chasing down your full potential. I will then share my own story to provide further insight. Having

---

[99] Wale, "Sunshine," Azlyrics,
http//:www.azlyrics.com/lyrics/wale/sunshine.html.

all this in mind, I must say that I am not the end all or be all of knowledge. We all have different ideas, principles and strategies for success. Please combine these strategies with your own.

Strategies

There are tons of books you can read that focus on how you can better yourself from the inside out. I think these concepts are important and we should always work on making ourselves better on the inside. I believe in this so much that I've read some of those books and have gone to therapy for several years. But I also believe there is a lack of books that help people understand the external powers and barriers that prohibit them from reaching their potential. The following strategies will help circumvent some of these crippling forces. They have worked for me, and I hope they work for you. The strategies are to get involved, understand the game and its players, play to your strengths, build your team, create and take advantage of initiatives and policies that benefit you and your community and lastly always be plannin'.

Get Involved

Maslow spent a lot of time studying people who reached self-actualization in his hierarchy. He found several common trends in these individuals. A trend that is important to note was that self-actualizing people were concerned and a part of a larger cause. This larger cause was found in their communities and/or around the world. I believe that in order for people to reach their higher selves they must find at least one issue or cause they're passionate about. To find what this issue or cause is for you, you should get involved with different groups and/or organizations until you find your fit.

Getting involved with groups and organizations allows you to discover and use your talents and skills. These talents and skills will be needed to explore your potential and to do the necessary tasks to reach it. Another reason to get involved is to increase your network, the number of people you know. The more people you know from different fields and backgrounds, the better your chances to achieve success. These people will assist you with obtaining resources, opportunities and information. All of these are needed to be successful. You see, I recognize that a part of being successful is a numbers game. The more people you know who are doing a variety of things will increase your opportunities. The more opportunities you take advantage of increase your likelihood of success.

The final reason to get involved is so dat you can learn the game. What I mean by this is that you can learn how people in the groups you get involved with use and channel power. This gives you the opportunity to learn and practice using power yourself.

Understand the game and its players

Our societies are governed by rules, rewards and outcomes like winners and losers. It's important to know the rules, cultures, norms and traditions of your environments. The thing I do reject from our societal structures is that there can only be winners or losers. I believe we all can be winners if we choose to create a society that uplifts everyone. But I digress. Since our social structures are governed by rules, laws, ordinances and legislations we are rewarded for following such rules and reprimanded if we do not. This dynamic of cause and effect can be compared to a game. Games like football, tennis and monopoly have rules. People are rewarded for playing by the rules and are reprimanded if they do not. The people who play the game the best win, for the most part. However, there are a lot of games aka structures, in society that are rigged and favor certain types of people. This is important to be aware of too. To get ahead in these games you have to, at minimum, try to understand the game or games that are being played around you. You also should pay attention to how they are being played. You have the right to play the game, or play at certain times or not play at all. My main point is to stay woke and be aware that people out here playing to the max.

To understand the game means that you are constantly watching and learning. You must identify the players, learn the rules, the lingo and ask questions. It's also important to find someone who you can trust who has been successfully playing so they can help you. Remember games are being played at your schools, colleges, communities, work place, religious institutions, programs, etc.

Let me give you an example. A game most of us played in school was going to class and trying to get a good grade. We know if you want a good grade you should attend most of your classes, do your work, participate and be on your best behavior. These are some of the things you need to do to get a good grade. But there are other things you can do to take your playin' of the game to the next level. You can meet and talk with your teacher. You can ask you teacher what are some other things you can do to be successful. You can ask for extra credit even if you don't need it and you can go to tutoring. The things that you do is how you play the game. Now, when I say people are playing the game to the max, means dat folks are not only doing the minimum to be successful but they are doing all the extra stuff. However, learning about the game isn't just knowing the rules and being cognizant of your level of play, but also taking notes of the other players and how they play the game.

Off bat, the person with the most power in the classroom is the teacher or professor. The teacher is the judge and referee. Your job is to study the teachers and find out how you can get on their good side. You also peepin' your classmates. You looking for which of your classmates already good with the teacher. Who takes great notes and who is getting in trouble? Once you have identified the players you will be watching how they play the game and their power moves. While you are gathering intel, you are playing your game but also makin' the necessary adjustments to what you observed. Then you move coordinately to your goal, which is to get a good grade.

We have established that power is the capacity to get what you want. This definition is important to remember when you are trying to understand the game. What is critically important is knowing the ways people and organizations go about getting what they want. These are the ways they express their power and/or capacity to get people to behave the way they want them to. Moisés Naím, author of *The End of Power from Boardrooms to Battlefields and Churches to States*, Why Being in Charge isn't What It Used to Be, does a great job explaining how power is expressed and channeled. Naím writes that power is expressed in four ways: muscle, the code, the pitch and the reward.[100] These channels are the ways people go about getting what they want.

The muscle is force or the threat of using force. Better known as coercion. Muscle can take the form of police force, getting fired from your job or being banished from your religious institution. The second way of expression

---

[100] Moisés Naím, *The End of Power From Boardrooms to Battlefields and Churches to States, Why Being in Charge isn't What it Used to Be* (New York: Basic Books, 2013), 23-25.

is the code, the rules we follow. They are our morals, cultural norms, traditions and social expectations. This "channel of power does not employ coercion; instead, it activates our sense of moral duty."[101] This shows up by people following the "Golden Rule" or when Muslims pray several times a day. The pitch is the third form of expression. "The pitch is just the capacity to persuade others to see the situation in a way that leads them to advance the persuader's goals and interest."[102] This can take the form of a company's advertisement or even when someone is spittin' game to convince another person to go on a date with them. The final channel is the reward. This is the ability to offer people coveted rewards as an advantage to get them to behave accordingly to the rewarder's interests and/or goals. This takes form when predominately white colleges and universities offer an accelerated tenure track to minority faculty because they want to enhance their curriculum and retain minority faculty and students. A personal example is when I'm visiting my parents' house and my mom cooks my favorite Haitian dishes because she wants me to stay home and not go out partying with my friends. My mom knows I love to eat! Keep in mind that people can use multiple channels at once to get what they want. It's your job to peep it and make the required adjustments.

Understanding the game can be compared to using Maslow's cognitive capacities to satisfy our needs.

---

[101] Ibid., 24.
[102] Ibid., 24.

Knowing how the different games are being played helps you figure how you will maintain or reach the next level of the hierarchy. You figuring out how the game is played helps you find the lane or lanes you will use to get where you wanna go.

Play to your strengths

Dr. Ruby Payne the author of *A Framework for Understanding Poverty* lists a set of strengths and resources people can use to better their circumstances.[103] She writes once the student and educator knows the student's strengths, then both can work together on finding or creating interventions that are congruent with the student's strengths. She uses a strength-based model, which I am a fan of. Dr. Payne's book focuses primarily on class and socioeconomics but I think the strengths she mentions can be adapted for our purposes. The strengths are "financial, emotional, mental/cognitive, spiritual, physical, support systems, relationships/role models, knowledge of hidden rules and language/formal register."[104]

The financial strength is having money to buy goods or services. This may mean you have the finances to buy books, materials, to travel, attend conferences and pay for tutoring. All of these things and more will assist you on

---

[103] Ruby K. Payne, *A Framework for Understanding Poverty A Cognitive Approach* (Highlands: aha! Process, Inc., 2013), 8-10.
[104] Ibid., 8.

your path of reaching your full potential. The second strength is emotional. "Emotional resources provide the stamina to withstand difficult and uncomfortable emotional situations and feelings."[105] In addition you won't self-sabotage or engage in unhelpful behaviors toward others. With this strength, you are able to deal with difficult situations and keep it movin'. It also means that you will be able to deal with uncomfortable and/or embarrassing social situations. The third type of strength is mental/cognitive.[106] This means that you can take in information, process it and use it in everyday life. You are able to read and access information from different sources and make sense of it. To use me, as an example, I've only taken two businesses in college but I run my own business. So, I read a lot of business articles, books and attend workshops to learn how to do business more effectively. Once I've taken in the information I apply it to my business. If something that I have learned doesn't work, I'll then try it differently or I'll research another method all together.

The fourth strength is spiritual. "Spiritual resources are the belief that help can be obtained from a higher power, that there is a purpose for living, and that worth and love are gifts from God."[107] I believe this is my strongest strength. The best thing my parents did for me was introducing me to God. This strength gives me hope

---

[105] Ibid., 9.
[106] Ibid.
[107] Ibid.

and a future story. I believe God has a purpose for me and God's prayer for me and to me is to reach that purpose to glorify the Lord's kingdom and help better the lives of others. My spiritual journey has expanded my thoughts about myself, the world and what I can do in this world. And most importantly I'm never on this journey alone. God has and will always be with me. To be clear, a spiritual resource isn't just the Christian religion. It's believing in a higher power that gives you hope and a future. That maybe the Muslim religion for some and Buddhism for others.

The next strength is physical, meaning that you are "capable and mobile."[108] This means you're pretty self-sufficient. It may also mean that you're athletic and good at sports. My good health allows me to move about and do different things with very little challenge. A message for you and for myself is to always take care of your body. Also, this world is built for those with fully mobile and healthy bodies, which oppresses those with different abilities. Ableism is a form of power that we must be conscious of.

The sixth strength is having a support system.[109] This resource is the people that have your back. They are there when you need them and they are able to help you emotionally. I call my support system my village because they been holding me down from day one. I can always

---

[108] Ibid.
[109] Ibid.

count on them for anything and if they can't help out they'll find someone who can. They have remained loyal to me and I to them. Side note: loyalty is not a word it's a way of life. The next strength is relationship/role models.[110] Role models help you learn how to live life. Role models are also mentors. Wherever you are in life, always try to find a mentor or someone you can emulate. Role models and mentors have been fundamental in my development and success. So, if this is a strength for you continue to use it and find other mentors as you move in different spaces in life. They can also help you with the next strength.

The eight strength is knowledge of hidden rules. "Hidden rules exist in poverty, in middle class, and in wealth, as well as in ethnic groups and other units of people. Hidden rules are about the salient, unspoken understandings that cue the members of the group that a given individual does or does not fit."[111] If this is your strength you are able to navigate within those particular groups really well. You can use this to your advantage by accessing the knowledge and resources that group has or controls. The final strength is language/formal register.[112] This strength is having the skills and a level of vocabulary mastery and writing in order to move through school and work successfully. I think of this strength like you are able to speak and write the King's or Standard English

---

[110] Ibid.
[111] Ibid., 10.
[112] Ibid.

efficiently. If this is your strength continue to use it and think of ways on how you can expand your work and network.

Playing to your strengths allows you to be true to yourself and offers you the ability to help others and organizations. You always gotta be thinking "where can I use my strengths and who can benefit from my strengths." And when you are using your strengths, you almost always gonna shine because you doing you! And doing you comes easy! Finally, playing to your strength can be viewed as using your individual power.

Pause: What are your strengths?

Build your Team

What I've learned from life is that you can't do it alone. As I think about my work and success I couldn't have done it all myself. I have found that building teams provides emotional and financial support, feedback and opportunities. In most facets of my life I have a group of people I can call and depend on for help. When I was growing up in South Florida I had tight knit groups that supported and influenced me. Till this day, we continue helping each other.

When I went to college I created close ties to several of my peers, professors, work colleagues and community leaders. These are the same people I continue working with. So, find people you connect with, you vibe with, and y'all share the same goals. These people must be committed to being positive and you all should be pushing each other to get better. Having teams allows you to share talents, skills, information, knowledge and resources. Finally, having a team or teams gives you access to others who will help you understand and navigate the social systems (the game) and powers that could keep you from reaching your potential.

Create & Take Advantage of Initiatives and Policies

I mentioned before that our societies are based on rules like local ordinances, laws and policies. These rules can be coupled with initiatives. In fact, initiatives, can be prerequisites to new rules. Initiatives can be the goals and/or plans of an organization and community. Such initiatives can be to better the health of community members, to clean up the environment, reduce substance abuse or increase diversity. It is your job to create and find out which rules and/or initiatives in your school, college, job and/or community benefit you. But before you can do that you have to have an idea of what your goals and interests are. Your goals and/or interests can be the things you want or the things you need to be successful. Knowing these things stem from you exploring yourself and reflecting on what you want out of life.

Check it, I'll explain this in one example. When I was in college I knew, I wanted to be an above average student. I wanted to graduate and get that paper. However, I wasn't working at my fullest capacity because I didn't know I was dyslexic and had learning differences. I also didn't know that the way we are traditionally educated isn't inclusive for all type learners. So, I mean I was achieving my goal but it wasn't my best effort. Once I was diagnosed and received the tools I needed I began to work at my fullest capacities. My grades shot up. Now, here's the kicker: colleges and universities must provide reasonable accommodations to persons with disabilities. This is covered under The American with Disabilities Act (ADA) of 1990 section 504.[113] It is the law. I took advantage of this federal law to achieve my goal. But I wouldn't have known or even used this law for my benefit if I didn't know my interests or if I wasn't willing to explore my identity of being a different learner.

You not only have to do your research on current laws and initiatives that will benefit you but you must put yourself in the position to create such laws and initiatives. This may mean joining student government at your school. You may have to join a committee at your job that you don't wanna join. It may require you to attend community meetings and volunteer. It's about putting yourself in the position to create laws and initiatives that will benefit you and your village. This is you actively

[113] American Psychological Association, "DART Toolkit II: Legal Issues – ADA Basics" *American Psychological Association*, http://www.apa.org/pi/disability/dart/legal/ada-basics.aspx.

using your power to design an environment for your success.

Always be plannin'

Growing up in South Florida my friends and I would say, "I'm plottin" or "you stay plottin." The former phrase means I'm devising a plan and the latter is you are always planning. I think in most facets of life a person should have a plan. I do a lot of planning with schools, organizations, small businesses, communities, non-profits, youth and with young professionals. Planning is critical in achieving goals. There are tons of planning models you can search on the internet or in books. The point is in order to navigate systems with competing powers you must be intentional and to be intentional you gotta have a plan. Here are some things to keep in mind while you are planning.

Set goals dat pushes your imagination about yourself and your capabilities, in this universe. Write all of your goals and dreams down. Create plans that are designed to achieve those goals and dreams. Be sure that your plan is true to you, your talents, strengths, skills and passions. Build your plan to be a part of your daily routine and make sure it's flexible enough to absorb changes, setbacks and opportunities. Be sure to take calculated risks and include some type of personal assessment to measure your achievement and well-being. Remember your team when you are planning and executing. Do not be afraid to fail. Do not be afraid to fail. Yea, I said it twice. Welcome failure and learn from it. Plan always to increase your network. Finally, always plan to take care of yourself. Self-care is so important and you can never plan too much of it. Whatever model of planning you use please keep these ideas in mind.

Story Time

It ain't easy being a young black man in this country. My Haitian friends and I would say la vi a di, which means life is hard. Growing up I wasn't really aware of my race, though. Most people around me were people of color. I mean, I knew racism existed but I didn't know what it truly meant. I was more aware of my ethnicity and what that meant because South Florida has so many different ethnic groups. I didn't fully understand the meaning of being black in America until I moved away for college. However, since my childhood and until now, I have been discriminated against and threatened because of my race. I've been called the n-word and insulted because of my race. I've been stereotyped and demeaned because of my race. Se bagay serye map diw (these are serious matters I'm telling you). I realized I wasn't dealt the best of cards. But I knew I couldn't give up. I had to be fighter like in the song by Gym Class Heroes and like my parents and extended family members.[114]

---

[114] Gym Class Heroes, "The Fighter," *Direct Lyrics,*
http://www.directlyrics.com/gym-class-heroes-the-figher-lyrics.html.

The thing that really worked for me when I was child was getting involved in extracurricular activities. I got involved at my church, school and community. Getting involved in school clubs, sports and community organizations were my outlet. I wasn't called dumb in these groups like in my classes or in the school hallways. Those programs allowed and pushed me to shine and I was praised by my peers and the adults. Those were the places where people started to tell me I had potential. I began to develop my leadership skills, which later became one of my strengths. The people in these programs would tell me that I could do so many things if I wanted. And that's what I did. I was a Sunday school teacher at my church and was involved with the youth ministry. I got involved in student councils from elementary school to high school and student government in college. I did theatre from elementary school to college. I really enjoyed acting and being a part of theatre productions. I got involved with the Navy Junior Reserve Officers Training Corps (NJROTC) and the drill team after I saw my older cousin in her JROTC uniform. I learned what it meant to be patriotic from the instructors of this program. I was a part of countless groups and each one contributed to my development. I also tried to play almost every sport that was available. But the organization I want to focus for our purposes is my work with county wide non-profit in Broward County.

When I was in elementary school I was a part of the Drug Abuse Resistance Education (D.A.R.E) program. As

I was leaving elementary school to middle school, my D.A.R.E officer told me he'd like for me to stay involved but there wasn't a D.A.R.E program at my middle school. He told me there was a similar program that I could join. I took his advice and joined a leadership and substance abuse prevention youth program. This youth program was a part of a county-wide non-profit and its mission was to strengthen communities throughout Broward County. The youth program was a county-wide initiative and it educated young people about leadership and the dangers of using drugs. It taught youth prevention methods we could use to educate our peers about substance abuse. This program was instrumental to my social development. I can talk for days on what this after school and out-of-school program did for me and my friends. I can talk for days on how the diverse staff from that program mentored us and how they continue to mentor us today. But I ain't got days.

I learned how to be a leader and how to lead at my school and in my communities. My peers and I worked on changing our county around issues that affected all people. As a leader in this program I got to meet and work with all kinds of people. I worked with police officers, teachers, doctors, lawyers, judges, business owners, newscasters, politicians and so many others. I really started to understand how my community worked and how to get things done within my community. By the time I was senior in high school, I was the president of this county-wide program and had been working in my community for about seven years. I wasn't able to articulate it then but I was learning how power worked and how power moved in my community. I learned that being a part of an organization and a part of a larger initiative allowed me access to people, places, and resources. It allowed me to be in certain places and spaces to hear information and gain knowledge that others were not aware of. As I got older I began to learn that information and knowledge were types of power, as well.

In the spring of 2004, I graduated high school and started college in the fall. But before, I went to college I told myself that I wasn't going to get involved my freshmen year. I wanted a break. Then again, my father had other plans. That summer, before I started college my father and I were visiting campus and going through freshmen orientation. We ran into the Director of Multicultural Affairs, Mr. Larry Ervin. We were excited to see another brown face because they were so few and far between. We started talking to him and my dad went on a rant of all the things I did back at home and told the Director to keep an eye on me and to make sure I got involved. OMG! It was so embarrassing. I said to myself there goes my plans for stayin' low. In retrospect, my dad did me a favor. Research shows that students who get involved at their institutions are more likely to stay, be successful and are satisfied with their college experience.[115] From there the clubs and organizations I joined were instrumental to my learning and success.

That fall I was on the football team and I joined two student organizations. These organizations were Black Student Association (BSA) and Student Government Association (SGA). I was a member of BSA and I was the freshmen class president in SGA. As a member of BSA and a player on the football team I quickly learned from the upperclassmen that minority students were having a hard time on campus and in the surrounding communities. As I spent more time on campus and in the community I started to agree with them. Time went on things got really intense on campus. Minority students would talk about how they were being unfairly treated in the classroom, on campus and in the nearby communities. I had those same complaints. By my junior year, I was a campus leader. I was the President of BSA and Junior Class President in SGA. I was a part of other groups like Intervarsity, the Dance Team (I'm not the best dancer), Step Team and member of several leadership and honor societies. I did one theatre production my freshmen year called *The Exonerated* and was working on the play *Romeo and Juliet* my junior year. I played the part of Romeo and I was playing my final year of football. At this time professors and administrators knew me or knew of me. I

---

[115] Alexander W. Astin, "Student Involvement: A Developmental Theory for Higher Education," Journal of College Student Development 25, no. 4 (1984): 523,
http://www.ydae.purdue.edu/LCT/HBCU/documents/Student_Involvement_A_Development_Theory_for_HE_Astin.pdf (accessed February 2, 2017).

had relationships with Directors, Deans and Vice Presidents. I was able to meet and talk with the President on several occasions. I'm not saying all of this to brag but to illustrate how important it is to get involved. My friends and I had the ear of people in positions of power. So, when overt racism and anti-semitic events happened that year on campus my friends and I were able to get the attention of those in power.

We wanted our campus to be more inclusive and to celebrate us for who we were. That wasn't happening. But we really didn't know how to change it. Our mentors, like Ms. Paula McGhee, Dr. Lee Davis, Dr. Luther McKinney and others showed us how. They taught us about social justice and how to create change. They taught us how institutions worked and what we should expect.

My major was history and I spent a lot of time researching and learning about the histories of marginalized people around the world. The institution itself valued social change and the curriculum had an emphasis on justice. My professors and classes taught us to support each other, know the facts and do our research. This increased our influence and leverage of power. My friends and I came up with a plan and proposed it to the campus community. The push back we received was heartbreaking. People who I thought were my friends started to act differently towards me and others members of BSA. I remember calling my friends and my dad crying. I told my dad how hard it was. My dad would say, "Bagay yo paka reta konsa", which meant things are not always going to be this way. He would tell me be strong and know God is with you. I commented to him this is what it means to be black in America. He would say, "Yea." He would follow up and say, "We have to keep pushing young man." I couldn't share these things with my mom because she would have worried too much. I stayed the course and by the end of my senior year the campus made some really good changes.

I graduated from my undergrad in 2008 and started working on my Masters. And of course, I ran into the same issues at my second institution. It was a PWI as well. My complexion was starting to feel real heavy. I got involved on campus and surrounded myself with likeminded graduate students. We really supported each other. Our mentors took the time to meet with us, plan with us and give sound advice on how to be successful in such of an environment. By this time, I learned that social justice was my passion and concentrated my studies on assisting underrepresented students and athletes. Students that were like me.

In my research during grad school I found that minority students experienced more trauma at PWIs then their white peers and a resource minority students could use on campus was the counseling center.[116] As I was

---

[116] Beth Rosenthal and Cody Wilson, "Mental Health Services: Use and Disparity Among Diverse College Students," Journal of American College Health 57, no. 1 (2008): 62,
http://www.web.ebscohost.com/ehost/pdf (accessed

doing this research I told myself I should try counseling. I went to counseling and I was paired with a black therapist. She was great! The counseling process was so helpful. It also helped me get through my last year of grad school. I graduated from my Master's program late spring of 2011. While I was searching for a job, I started my consulting firm. I realized in grad school that there were very few colleges and universities around the country that were fully inclusive in their educational practices and policies. So, I started my firm around this need and worked on it part-time. I found a job in New Hampshire and I left Tennessee that summer. However, things didn't change much at the institution where I received my Masters. In fact, the state legislators recently defunded diversity initiatives.[117]

In New Hampshire, I quickly found out that the working force wasn't no joke! It was a whole different game I had to learn. It too was a PWI. When I got to my job, I spent time learning and observing my environment. I did this by asking questions and attended a number of functions and events. I then got involved on several committees. By doing these things I was not only able to learn about my environment but I also learned about the institution from different perspectives. After some time, I

February 1, 2017).

[117] Megan Boehnke, "UT Disbands Diversity Office Eliminates Four Positions," *Knoxville News Sentinel,* May 20, 2016, accessed November 18, 2016, http://www.archive.knoxnews.com/news/local/ut-disbands-diversity-office-eliminates-four-positions-334868cd-f50c-120d-e053-01000007fa864-380288111.html.

learned who were the major players and how power flowed in the organization.

I really did enjoy that job but the college lacked diversity. I started to realize that some of my white colleagues didn't know how to take me. At that time, I was the only young black male student affairs professional in the whole organization. People were not use to seeing a young, educated and talented man of color. I got a strange vibe from people which I still have a hard time explaining. But my office was doing a great job. The Vice President of Student Affairs, who was one of my supervisors, commended us on our work at the annual department wide meeting. We were achieving all of our goals despite getting constant push back from other offices. People around campus commended us on our work also. But my students and I never felt fully accepted.

Then one day, at the latter part of my tenure there, I was walking home from work. As I was walking on the street I lived on some white guys angrily yelled the n-word at me. It was out of nowhere. I turned around to say something but by mid-turn I realized that they knew where I lived. We lived on same block. They were literally across the street from me. I continued in my originally direction and I didn't say anything. After that moment, I increasingly got worried about my safety and my home. When I got into my apartment I told myself, "I gotta get out of here!"

At the time, I stayed in touch with my mentors. I had a long-time mentor, Joe Toliver, the CEO of Dooling Enterprise. He told me during grad school that I belonged working on the national level. Mr. Toliver had known me since middle school. He and his colleagues Reverend Jones, Shahara Jaghoo, Pat Castillo and others taught me everything about community work and community change. Mr. Toliver was like you have that kind potential to work on the national level and you need to move to the Washington D.C. area. And to tell you the truth I didn't believe him. It was already a struggle for me to get the job that I had. The struggle was real. So, to think of doing work on the national level didn't seem to be in my reach. From Maslow's perspective, I couldn't think of working on the national level to reach my potential because I was more concerned about my safety. I was using my cognitive capacities to meet my safety needs. Another reason was that my self-esteem wasn't high enough for me to think I could do well on that level.

Time went on and things did not get better. Then God instructed me to move to the DMV (D.C., Maryland, Virginia) area. In the spring of 2013, I resigned from my position and moved to the DMV with my sister. Since then that institution has made some really positive changes around diversity.

When I moved, I didn't have a job. I had several interviews but nothing worked out. It was a tough time. I was doing some consulting but I didn't have full time work. I applied to job after job after job. I wasn't getting any looks and my business mentors, Mr. Toliver and Mr. Earl Coleman CEO of Pearlio, LLC a branding company, suggested that I focus on the consulting firm full time. I took their advice. I was also able to get a part job working as an adjunct professor at the University of the District of Columbia.

I placed most of my efforts into building my business but I wasn't aware that the DMV had a large population of minority business owners. There were a large number of educated and talented minority business owners doing their thang. I was no longer an anomaly. There were people like me doing similar things. I realized what Eric Thomas the Hip-Hop Preacher meant by "go to the places you are celebrated and not just tolerated."[118] I started to learn the game aka the business environment. I learned that minority businesses were valued (for the most part) and were successful in the area. I learned that there were a slew of government incentives and laws that favor minority, women and small businesses. I took advantages of the low-cost business workshops, events and conferences in the area. By this time, I was training and consulting nationally and internationally. I was finally in a place where my race wasn't the thing that was mostly scrutinized. I was living in an area and working with organizations that made me to feel safe and valued. This allowed my hierarchy of needs to change and I desired to

[118] Tito Kang, "1 Step to Happiness!," *Unlock The Leader's Kode,* 27 May 2011, http://www.titokang.com/happiness-2/qwyk-typs-1-step-to-happiness/

obtain the higher levels of Maslow's hierarchy. I was no longer worried about my safety. I was working on my belonging and esteem needs. I can only describe where I was by a Wale verse. He stated, "although I hit my stride, ain't even in prime (nah)."[119] I felt like I could freely be myself (for the most part) and I could push myself to my max without any major contrasting powers or barriers in my way. When I came to this realization it was liberating!

Conclusion

It's only right that I share some of the limitations of my argument. The theories I used for the foundations of my thesis are from a Western perspective and do not encompass the complexity of other cultures and thinkers from different parts of the world. Therefore, my arguments will not work in all cultures. I will release a more global book in the future. The length of this book doesn't allow me to cover many topics extensively, which requires you to do your own research. I have not covered current psychological theory or research and/or the critiques of Maslow and Lukes' theories. However, even with these limits I hope this book speaks to you, to your power and to your dreams.

I hope that you have realized and/or have been validated by the fact that we all have power. I believe we all have the capacity and power to get what we want out

---

[119] Wale, "Sunshine Lyrics," *Metro Lyrics*
http://www.metrolyrics.com/sunshine-lyrics-wale.html.

of life. I believe all people are capable of doing good and achieving success. However, our power, your power are strings among many others. Our powers and the powers around us are tied together an elaborate set of complex entangled webs. Within these webs are supporting, contrasting and neutral powers. Our lives, who we are, where we were born and so many other factors place us in a certain part of this network of webs. Ultimately, if our power is tied to each other than the same is for our potential.

A question I keep asking myself while thinking about these webs of power is, "Can oppressed people truly reach their full potential, within an oppressed system?" In this network of webs my oppression and power are tied to each other. This reminds of a quote by Audre Lorde, which I read while visiting the Smithsonian National Museum of African American History & Culture (#APeoplesJourney) on its opening weekend. It was such blessing to be there at that moment. Audre Lorde a writer and feminist wrote, "I recognized that my power as well as my primary oppressions come as result of my blackness as well as my womanness, and therefore my struggles on both of these fronts are inseparable."[120] She recognized that her oppression and power are tied to her identities. Since these things are tied together, sometimes it's hard for me to believe that we can truly reach our pinnacle selves. The oppression holds us down. You know me, I can get real

---

[120] Wall Text, *History*, National Museum of African American History and Culture, Washington, D.C.

pessimistic sometimes. But what would it mean to believe the oppressed could never be fully realized? Langston Hughes wrote a poem about Dreams. The poem goes.

> Hold fast to dreams
> For if dreams die
> Life is a broken-winged bird
>
> That cannot fly.
>
> Hold fast to dreams
> For when dreams go
> Life is a barren field
> Frozen with snow.[121]

To believe that we aren't able to obtain our wildest dreams and dat we cannot become the best versions of ourselves is to live a broken, barren and cold life. This is what a system of oppression wants and what it accomplishes every day. People are living broken lives with forgotten dreams. The band The Script has great song titled Superheroes.[122] And like in that song we must use and/or turn our pains and struggles into our power. However, we can't do it alone. We must help each other. I believe if we work together and believe in something greater we can begin tapping into our greater selves. For me personally I believe we were made in God's image. Therefore, being human isn't just flesh and blood. It means a part of being

---

[121] Langston Hughes, "Dreams," *Poets.org*,'
http://www.poets.org/poetsorg/poem/dreams.
[122] The Script, "Superheroes," *Genius*,
http://www.genius.com/The-script-superheroes-lyrics.

a full human being is also being a spirit because we are an extension of a spiritual being. Hence, when I think of my own power it doesn't only come from myself or this world. It comes from something greater which gives me courage and strength. Gospel artist Travis Greene has a song titled Made a Way.[123] In this song God uses heavenly power to make a way for us. God removes barriers for our success.

Again, I ain't tryin' to preach to you, just telling you how I feel. We need each other because this individual stuff ain't working. Our potentials are tied to one another as is our power. We cannot continue to allow opposing powers to negatively affect our potential and dreams. As people let's turn #NoEntry to #Access. Let's power up our potential so we may prosper!

So, as you continue through life, living, remember to always believe in yourself, find and allow others to believe in you and find something to believe in! Live life to the fullest and be sure to live you to the fullest! "We gon' be alright!"[124]

The only thing now to do…is…bust a move!

Pause: What's your game plan?

---

[123] Travis Greene, "Made a Way Lyrics," *Metro Lyrics,*
http://www.metrolyrics.com/made-a-way-lyrics-greene.html.
[124] Kendrick Lamar, "Alright," *Genius,*
http://www.genius.com/Kendrick-lamar-alright-lyrics.

NO ENTRY

Afterword

I cannot tell you how many times I've read Carter G. Woodson's seminal volume titled, "The Mis-Education of the Negro." Probably a half dozen or more and, of course, that does not include the 50 or so times that I have referenced the book or skimmed its precious pages in search of a particular excerpt or quote for a book chapter, keynote, or Sunday morning sermon. For example, many will be familiar with Woodson's cogent analysis of how damaging and paralyzing psychological control can be when he wrote: "If you can control a man's thinking you do not have to worry about his action. When you determine what a man shall think you do not have to concern yourself about what he will do." So much truth in that timeless passage. And although parents, preachers, and many speakers have direct-quoted, mis-quoted, or alluded to similar sentiments many times throughout my life, I haven't always been aware that Dr. Carter G. Woodson was the author of this observation. Moreover, I certainly didn't know the context in which the statement was made—as part of Woodson's critique of the educational experiences of Black Americans at the time.

Speaking of, I am not entirely sure when I first encountered mention of Dr. Carter Godwin Woodson. I guess it's possible that I heard of him during Black History Month, growing up in the suburbs of Virginia Beach but, quite honestly, my teachers didn't devote a memorable amount of classroom time to discussing the history and contributions of Black Americans to society. I remember a few furtive "pedagogical glances" at Dr. Martin Luther King, Jr., Malcolm X, and Rev. Jesse Jackson. Most of these lessons were quick, fleeting and never required a substantive investigation of the life contributions of such multidimensional Black leaders. No major keynote speakers. No long essays or papers. And virtually no mention of modern-day Black leaders who were making a difference to change the material conditions of Black Americans in Virginia Beach (my hometown), Virginia (my home state), or the world.

I have vivid memories of relatively short conversations about Dr. Martin Luther King, Jr—usually the same spread of facts—verbal review of his resume as a Black preacher, father, civil rights leader, and, by subtle implication, a fiery orator, which became obvious once we silently listened to an excerpt of King's famous "I Have a Dream" speech. I use the phrase "by subtle implication" in the spirit of complete transparency to point out the fact that in over 12 years of public education at award-winning schools within a highly-regarded school district—known for graduating high-achieving, college ready kids—I cannot recall a single instance where a teacher or administrator praised Dr. King as a gifted orator, a public intellectual, a masterful artist, or even an exemplar worthy of academic study in communications, public speaking, or literature. No, instead, I learned what all other students learned and I came to expect what all other students expected—a quick review of Dr. King's entire life and legacy during a 2-minute soundbite and 7-minute PBS (Public Broadcasting Service) video in the month of February that starts with his birth on January 15, 1929, highlights his role as a son of a Black southern preacher, his marriage to (the now late) Corretta Scott King, his efforts to organize and lead the March on Washington that took place August 28, 1963, and his untimely death on the balcony of the Lorraine Hotel in Memphis, Tennessee on April 4, 1968, just after delivering his prophetic "Mountaintop" speech at Mason Temple Church of God in Christ (COGIC) the night before. It wasn't until much later—and usually through out-of-school educative experiences—that I learned about Dr. King's children, death threats from the Klu Klux Klan (KKK), wire-tapping of his phones, and daunting governmental resistance to King's call for more nonviolent protests that strove to usher in a day when all God's children would be "free at last." With each new discovery about King's life, and Malcolm X's life, and Bayard Rustin's life, and…well, you get my point…I wondered why none of this had been discussed or presented during my 12 years of public education in award-winning schools within a well-resourced school district in Virginia.

It would be several years after high school graduation, as an undergraduate at the University of Virginia (UVA), that I felt compelled to read Carter G. Woodson's Mis-Education in its entirety. There were at least two reasons for my commitment to make it through the entire book.

First, I was curious about the namesake especially since his name is proudly displayed on a building at UVA: The Carter G. Woodson Institute for Afro-American and African Studies, which was founded in 1981. Second, my interest in education and educational disparities had evolved although my ability to articulate the underlying causal mechanisms of such inequities was significantly underdeveloped. One of the professors in the UVA Curry School of Education told me to read Carter G. Woodson's book: "It will help you frame the problem you're trying to address. It will give you the language that you need." And with that advice, I picked up a copy of the book from Barnes & Noble, cuddled up with a warm cup of coffee, and started to read.

I wasn't a full two chapters in before I realized that I had been miseducated. Now, before I go too far into my argument here, let me calm the anxiety of those who think this is my late-coming attempt to publicly shame and disgrace the elementary, middle (then, "junior high"), and high schools that I attended. Like Woodson, I am not pointing out "my schools" as isolated examples of the pervasive miseducation that takes place in the country—no, miseducation is a far more insidious, institutionalized ill that affects schools and districts and kids across the globe. But, after reading a few chapters of Woodson's Mis-Education, I found myself nodding in agreement with his critique of an educational system in the United States that fails to present authentic Black (then, "Negro") history in school.

Woodson's analysis helped me identify and problematize books and "standardized"[125] curricula that only contain causal references to Blacks in America, especially those "educational materials" that restrict representations of Black Americans to menial, subordinate roles, always inferior to "White greatness" or "fortunate enough" to serve "White masters in the house" while their darker-skinned Black kinfolk were happy to pick cotton for their master in the field. Woodson helped me become consciously frustrated, dissatisfied with popular images of Black slaves that subtly (and not-so-subtly) cast Blacks as less than human or photos that rendered them (that is, "us") as nothing more than caricatures of laziness, tired, shiftless, uneducated, and unambitious. Despite all the resources available to them within the district and all the degrees and credentials of the teachers in my schools, thanks to Woodson, I too "woke up" to the fact that I had received this impoverished education about Black Americans, myself, and our history that was littered with hiccups in the recall of real Black history. An impoverished education about Black Americans, myself, and our history that was laced with lies or at least intentionally (and perhaps at times unintentionally) distorted facts about slavery and segregation (what many today would call "Alternative Facts"). An impoverished education about Black

---

[125] Quotes within this paragraph are my own and I use the symbol (") to mark off terms that masquerade in educational spaces as objective or fair, although they themselves are part of the miseducation that Blacks receive.

Americans, myself, and our history that was lined with flimsy justifications for social pathologies such as slavery, racism, classism as necessary conditions for maintaining "a more perfect Union." I had been miseducated and now I had to do something about it.

Now a social scientist at a major research university in the Midwestern region of the United States, I consciously work to do something about miseducation. No, I don't always organize protests and marches, campaigns or revolts, but my woke activism is not less significant. I conduct research and publish journal articles, chapters, and books on Black education revealing the sizable disparities that perpetuate limited or "no entry" for Black students to college, graduate school, and careers. For instance, we know and I call out in my research that the United States spends more money per full-time student than other OECD countries. Moreover, the U.S. spends on-average $334 more on every White student compared to non-White student. Of course, spending differentials of that kind accumulate over a lifetime such that the U.S. spends over $2000 more on every White student during their first 6 years in school, compared to their same-ability, non-White peers. What's fair about that? And, then when the young Black male is reading one or two grade levels behind by the 4th grade, why do we scratch our heads, wonder why, and then blame him and his family?! This reinforces the point that Colber Prosper and others make about the devastating blow that power can have on one's life chances and educational trajectory.

As a human scientist in the College of Education and Human Ecology at The Ohio State University, I consciously work to do something about miseducation by restoring the humanity of marginalized and oppressed populations and giving voice—yes, power—back to the people. I am driven to restore humanity (and dignity) to those who have for too many years and too many reasons been dehumanized by researchers through the numbing use of mathematical/statistical symbols (e.g., X, y, N, %) and the imposition of strict standards and variable names that render some groups "too small to be counted" or "too few to really matter." So, although I was trained as a quantitative methodologist in techniques and tools that aligned with my propensity toward math, numbers, and "how many, how much" curiosities, I saw the need for different, new approaches that enabled me to uncover the story, the cause for the pause (or anxious stutter), the trigger for the tears or outburst of laughter. I developed stronger skills in and understanding of qualitative methods after completing my PhD because they equipped me to activate my own activism by giving voice to the experiences of those who are rarely heard in the published literature like Black males, first-generation college students, economically disadvantaged students, Black women, gay men of color, and those who live at the intersection of these and myriad social identities. I see myself addressing miseducation by rewriting wrongs and completing incomplete analyses through my research that uses power and powerful tools to give power back to people who are powerful in and of themselves, without which they would have "no entry" as Colber Prosper has mentioned herein.

Like Colber Prosper, one of my former students, one of my lifelong protégés, and "forever friends," I too believe in the unimaginable. I believe in the boundless possibilities of human creativity and talent. I believe that all kids, all students, and all people can achieve greatness as they define it when they are provided with equitable opportunities and appropriate support. Our collective potential, as a country, is far too great to deny the inequities of our educational system that strip far too many kids of such opportunities to achieve their dream. We must admit that there are serious problems that offer little to "no entry" for some segments of our population to move upward socially, to attend college regularly, or to enjoy life, liberty, and the pursuit of happiness. Of course, admitting the problem is just half the battle. Then we must do the hard work of identifying the cause of such inequities, evaluate plausible solutions for reducing and ultimately eliminating such barriers to success, and then work to implement the most effective solutions that demonstrably fix what's been broken for many, many years. I'll start with an admission too: What I outline is really hard work. But, hard work has never been excuse for retreat. Let's all join Prosper and others across the globe in doing the "good work" of hard work!

-Terrell Strayhorn, Ph.D.
Professor, Researcher, Provocateur

CPSIA information can be obtained
at www.ICGtesting.com
Printed in the USA
LVOW11s1537111117
555908LV00001B/255/P